John Greenleaf Whittier

THE EARLY POEMS

OF

JOHN GREENLEAF WHITTIER

WITH

BIOGRAPHICAL SKETCH

BY

N. H. DOLE

NEW YORK
THOMAS Y. CROWELL & CO.
PUBLISHERS

CONTENTS.

iii

CONTENTS.

JOHN GREENLEAF WHITTIER.

BIOGRAPHICAL SKETCH.

CIRCUMSTANCES determine the poet; inheritance determines who the poet shall be. It somehow seems to be a marvellous thing that a thrifty, plain Quaker stock should come to such a flowering as was seen in John Greenleaf Whittier. That iridescent colors should play over the Quaker drab! That from the insignificant chrysalis should emerge the brilliant butterfly! From Keltic origin one might expect any surprises. Boyle O'Reilly, who had also something of the prophetic spirit, who also threw himself generously into conflict with powers that did their best to crush him and make a martyr of him, is explained by the fact that he was Keltic. But one scarcely expects a singer from the ranks of sober Friends. That is an anomaly; and to explain the phenomenon one must look into Whittier's ancestry.

Four steps bring us back to the days of the Puritans. Whittier's father, John, born in 1760, was the tenth child of Joseph, born in 1716, the ninth and youngest son of Joseph, born in 1669, who was in turn the tenth and youngest child of Thomas, who

was born in Southampton, England, in 1620, and
sailed for America in the good ship "Confidence"
a little more than two and a half centuries ago.
Thomas Whittier was no common man. He settled
on the Merrimack River, first in Salisbury, then in
old Newbury, then in Haverhill, where he built the
house in which his famous descendant was born.
He is said to have brought the first hive of bees to
Haverhill. In those days Indians frequently scalped
and murdered defenceless families of white settlers;
but Thomas Whittier made them his friends and
disdained to protect his house with flint-lock or
stockade.

Thomas Whittier's son, Joseph, married the daughter of the Quaker, Joseph Peasley, and thus the strain
which in those days was regarded as a disgrace, but
which in time became a mark of distinction, was
grafted upon the Whittier stock. The poet's grand-
father married Sarah Greenleaf, a descendant of a
French exile, whose name, instead of being perverted
like the *Lummydews* (L'Hommedieux) and the *De-
sizzles* (Des Isles), was simply translated into English. What part this Gallic blood played in Whittier's mental make-up, it would be no less difficult
than interesting to determine.

Whittier's mother, Abagail Hussey, was descended
from the Rev. Stephen Bachelor or Batchelder of
Hampton, N.H., a man who was famed for his
"splendid eye." This feature, which is generally
associated with genius, seemed to have been in-
herited by Whittier, and Daniel Webster, and William Pitt Fessenden, and Caleb Cushing. Dark,

expressive, penetrating eyes, full of soul and flashing with sudden lightning glances, were characteristic of the "Bachelder eye," common to so many families in New Hampshire.

Whittier's father married at the age of forty-four and had only four children, Mary, John Greenleaf, who was born September 17, 1807, Matthew Franklin, and Elizabeth Hussey.

The old Whittier farmhouse, with its huge central chimney, faces the south; the front lower rooms are square, with fifteen-inch oaken beams supporting the low ceilings. The poet was born in the west front room, the two small-paned windows of which look down to a little brook, which in those early days, says Whittier, "foamed, rippled, and laughed" behind its natural fringe of bushes. Across the way was the big unpainted barn. The scenery was the typical landscape of New England — a smooth, grassy knoll (known as Job's Hill), woodland composed of oaks, walnuts, pines, firs, and spruces, with sumachs, which in the autumn, and in the spring as well, are gorgeous with many colors. Whittier, however, was color blind, and all that splendid display counted as naught to him.

Behind the house was the orchard, and behind the orchard a clump of oaks, near which the Whittier graveyard used to be.

In 1798 the farm was rated as worth $200. The year before the poet was born his father bought one of three shares in it for $600 of borrowed money, and the debt was not cleared for a quarter of a century. Money was scarce in those days. And yet

John Whittier was honored by his townspeople, was frequently in the public service, and entertained men of note at his humble fireside.

When Whittier was seven years old, he went to school. His first teacher, who was his lifelong friend, was Joshua Coffin of old Newbury.

> Still sits the school-house by the road,
>   A ragged beggar sunning;
> Around it still the sumachs grow,
>   And blackberry vines are running.
>
> Within, the master's desk is seen,
>   Deep scarred by raps official;
> The warping floor, the battered seats,
>   The jack-knife's carved initial.
>
> The charcoal frescos on its wall;
>   The door's worn sill betraying
> The feet that, creeping slow to school,
>   Went storming out to playing.

It stood about half a mile from Whittier's home, but the fount of knowledge flowed during only about three months in the year.

At home the library was scanty. Only twenty books or so, mostly journals and memoirs of pious Quakers, furnished the boy home reading. He would walk miles to borrow a volume of biography or travel. Naturally, the precepts of the Bible, which was daily read, became a part of his mental and moral fibre. His poems are full of references to Bible events and characters. "In my boyhood," he says, "in our lonely farmhouse, we had scanty sources of information, few books, and only a small weekly newspaper. Our only annual was the Almanac. Under such circumstances story-telling was a necessary resource in the long winter evenings."

When Nature sets about to make a poet, she has her own college. These apparent deprivations are enrichments. They concentrate genius. The few hours of regular schooling were counterbalanced with lessons from Dame Nature herself.

> Knowledge never learned of schools,
> Of the wild bee's morning chase,
> Of the wild-flower's time and place,
> Flight of fowl and habitude
> Of the tenants of the wood;
> How the tortoise bears his shell,
> How the woodchuck digs his cell,
> How the ground-mole sinks his well;
> How the robin feeds her young,
> How the oriole's nest is hung;
> Where the whitest lilies blow,
> Where the freshest berries grow,
> Where the ground-nut trails its vine,
> Where the wood-grape's clusters shine;
> Of the black wasp's cunning way,
> Mason of his walls of clay,
> And the architectural plans
> Of gray hornet artisans;
> For eschewing books and tasks,
> Nature answers all he asks!
> Hand in hand with her he walks,
> Face to face with her he talks.

He goes on autobiographically : —

> I was rich in flowers and trees,
> Humming-birds and honey-bees;

> For my sport the squirrel played,
> Plied the snouted mole his spade;
> For my taste the blackberry cone
> Purpled over hedge and stone;
> Laught the brook for my delight
> Through the day and through the night,
> Whispering at the garden wall,
> Talkt with me from fall to fall;
> Mine the sand-rimmed pickerel pond;
> Mine the walnut slopes beyond,
> Mine, on bending orchard trees,
> Apples of Hesperides.

There was scanty time for play, however; that perpetual interest was eating up the meagre products of the farm; boys had to put their hands to the plough. "At an early age," he says, "I was set at work on the farm and doing errands for my mother, who, in addition to her ordinary house duties, was busy in spinning and weaving the linen and woollen cloth needed for the family."

The family was large, consisting, says Whittier, of "my father, mother, my brother and two sisters, and my uncle and aunt, both unmarried." In addition there was the district school-master, who boarded with them.

For graphic pen-pictures of this group, one must go to "Snow-Bound." There we shall see Uncle Moses, with whom the boys delighted to go fishing in the dancing brook.

His aunt, Miss Hussey, had the reputation of making the best squash pies that were ever baked. The influence of pie in developing character must not be overlooked. What oatmeal was to Carlyle, what the haggis was to Burns, the pie was to the true New Englander. It will not be forgotten how fond Emerson was of pie. Indigestion and poetry have a certain strange alliance; did not Byron purposely exacerbate his stomach in order to coin "Don Juan" into guineas?

Each member of that delightful household stands forth in living lines. "Snow-Bound" now needs no praise. It has been accepted as the typical idyl of a New England winter, the sweetest flower of New England home life.

It is greater than "The Cotter's Saturday Night" because it was written more from the heart. It stands with "The Cotter's Saturday Night" and, though, quite unlike, may have been inspired by Burns's immortal poem. To Burns, Whittier owed his first inspiration, and he himself tells how he learned first to know the Scotch poet. A wandering Scotchman came one day to the Whittier farmhouse. "After eating his bread and cheese and drinking his mug of cider, he gave us 'Bonnie Doon,' 'Highland Mary,' and 'Auld Lang Syne.' He had a full rich voice and entered heartily into the spirit of his lyrics."

When he was fourteen, Joshua Coffin brought a volume of Burns's poems, and read some of them, greatly to his delight. Says Whittier: "I begged him to leave the book with me, and set myself at once to the task of mastering the glossary of the Scottish dialect to its close. This was about the first poetry I had ever read (with the exception of that of the Bible, of which I had been a close student), and it had a lasting influence upon me. I began to make rhymes myself, and to imagine stories and adventure." When pen and ink failed him, he resorted to chalk or charcoal, and he hid away his effusions with the care with which a cat hides her young kittens.

It is interesting to know that recently one or two of Whittier's first attempts in rhyme, in Scotch dialect and in the manner of Burns, have been discovered.

When Whittier was in his eighteenth year, that is, in 1825, he wrote several poems which found their way the following year to the Newburyport *Free Press*, then just established by William Lloyd Garrison. The Whittiers subscribed for it, and in the "Poets' Corner" appeared in print the first of the young man's published verses, entitled "The Exile's Departure," written in the meter of "The Old Oaken Bucket." It is noticeable that the Exile sings : —

> Farewell, shores of Erin, green land of my fathers,
>   Once more and forever, a mournful adieu.

It would seem that Thomas Moore's Irish melodies must have fallen into his hands. The trace of Whittier's reading is often to be found in his poems. "Mogg Megone" also shows the insidious influence of "Lalla Rookh." "The Bridal of Pennacook" is Wordsworth, pure and simple, the praise of whom betrays its origin ; but not as yet, and not until long afterwards, did he succeed in attaining felicity in epithet. It was also the day of the Scott and of the Byron fever, and Whittier did not escape it.

It is said that Whittier was mending fences when the carrier brought the paper that contained his first printed lines and the editorial notice: "If W. at Haverhill will continue to favor us with pieces beautiful as the one inserted in our poetical department of to-day, we shall esteem it a favor." Whittier could hardly believe his eyes. He accepted the invitation. The second of his *Free Press* poems was in blank verse and entitled "Deity." He confided the secret to his sister. She informed Garrison that it was her brother who wrote them. One day when the young poet was hoeing in the cornfield, clad only in shirt, trousers, and straw hat, he was summoned into the house to see a visitor. It proved to be Garrison, who had driven over from Newburyport to make the acquaintance of his contributor. He insisted that Whittier showed such talent that he ought to have further education.

Whittier's father remonstrated against putting notions into the lad's head. "Sir," he said, "poetry will not give him bread." Besides, there was no money and no prospect of money. Suddenly a way opened. A young hired man knew how to make ladies' shoes and slippers. He offered to teach the art to his employer's son. Mr. Moses Emerson, one of Whittier's early teachers, used to relate how Whittier worked at his shoemaking in a little shop which stood in the yard, and how he sat on a bench amid tanned hides, pincers, bristles, paste pots, and rosin, stitching for dear life.

During the following winter he earned by it enough money to buy a suit of clothes and pay for six months' schooling at the new Academy in Haverhill. Whittier wrote the ode that was sung at the dedication of the new building. He boarded at the house of Mr. A. W. Thayer, editor and publisher of the Haverhill *Gazette*. Naturally the young poet contributed also to this paper some of his verses. He was now nineteen, and was long remembered as " a very handsome, distinguished-looking young man " with remarkably handsome eyes ; tall, slight, and very erect, bashful but never awkward.

Whittier used to like to relate the story of his first visit to Boston. He was dressed in a new suit of homespun, which for the first time were adorned with " boughten buttons." He expected to spend a week with the Greenes, who were family connections. Shortly after his arrival he sallied forth to see the sights. He described how he wandered up and down the streets, but somehow found it different from what he expected. The crowd was worse on Washington Street, and he soon got tired of being jostled and thought he would step aside into an alley-way and wait till " the folks " got by. But there was no cessation of the " terrible stream of people," some of whom stared at him with curious or mocking eyes. He stayed there a long time and began to be " lonesome."

At last, however, he mustered courage to leave his " coign of vantage," and safely reached Mrs. Greene's in time for tea. She had guests, among them a gay young woman whose beauty and vivacity especially interested him. But she began to talk about the theatre, and finally asked him to be present that evening. She was the leading lady! Whittier had promised his mother that he would never enter a playhouse. He was terribly shocked at the danger which he had run. He could not sleep that night, and next morning he took the early stage-coach for his country home. In after years he told this story with great zest, but he never broke the promise which he made to his mother.

At the close of the term, Whittier taught the district school at West Amesbury, thus enabling him to return for another six months at the Academy. Garrison had meantime gone to Boston, and through his influence Whittier secured a place there at a salary of nine dollars a week on the *American Manufacturer*. But this engagement was of short duration. In 1830 he was editing the Haverhill *Gazette*. He was beginning to be widely known as a poet. Next he became editor of the *New England Weekly Review* of Hartford, Conn., to which he also contributed upwards of forty poems, besides sketches and tales in prose. He boarded at the Exchange Coffee House, and lived a solitary, sedentary life. His health even then was delicate. At this time, if ever, occurred the hinted romance of his life. Writing of a visit to his home, he said: "I can say that I have clasped more than one fair hand, and read my welcome in more than one bright eye." More than one love-poem dated from this time. Long afterwards he touched upon these episodes in "Memories" and in "A Sea-dream." But Whittier never married.

He published his first volume in 1831, — "Legends of New England," a collection of his prose and verse. This was afterwards suppressed, as well as his first

narrative poem, "Moll Pitcher," published the following year. So far, with much promise, he had as yet
shown little originality. He bade fair to be simply a
poet. But two years later he took part in an event
which was destined to change the face of all things,
not for him alone, but for his country. In 1833 he
helped to organize the American Anti-slavery Society.
Henceforth, during a whole generation, his life was
to be a warfare: —

> Our fathers to their graves have gone;
> Their strife is past, their triumph won;
> But sterner trials wait the race
> Which rises in their honored place, —
> A moral warfare with the crime
> And folly of an evil time.
> So let it be. In God's own might
> We gird us for the coming fight.
> And, strong in Him whose cause is ours
> In conflict with unholy powers,
> We grasp the weapons He has given, —
> The Light and Truth and Love of Heaven.

Side by side with William Lloyd Garrison stood
Whittier. The manifesto of the one was the inspiration of the other: "I will be harsh as truth and as
uncompromising as justice. I am in earnest; I will
not equivocate; I will not excuse; I will not retreat
a single inch, and I will be heard!"

Whittier in the same spirit sang: —

> It we have whispered truth, whisper no longer;
> Speak as the tempest does, sterner and stronger;
>
> Still be the tones of truth louder and firmer,
> Startling the haughty South with the deep murmur;

> God and our charter's right, Freedom forever,
> Truce with oppression, never, Oh, never!

Nor would he allow the charms of mere literature to beguile him into pleasant paths. Putting aside melancholy, sentimental yearnings, he resisted the temptation, as he pathetically sings in the poem entitled " Ego."

The question of slavery began to be borne in upon him even before he settled in Hartford. On his return home he made a thorough study of the subject and wrote a twenty-three page pamphlet entitled " Justice and Expediency; or, Slavery Considered with a View to its Rightful and Effectual Remedy, — Abolition." It was printed at Haverhill at his own expense. Its argument was never answered. It concluded with this eloquent peroration : —

" And when the stain on our own escutcheon shall be seen no more; when the Declaration of Independence and the practice of our people shall agree; when Truth shall be exalted among us; when Love shall take the place of Wrong; when all the baneful pride and prejudice of caste and color shall fall forever; when under one common sun of political Liberty the slave-holding portions of our Republic shall no longer sit like Egyptians of old, themselves mantled in thick darkness while all around them is glowing with the blessed light of freedom and equality — then and not till then shall it GO WELL FOR AMERICA."

This preceded and led to his appointment as one of the delegates of the great Anti-slavery Convention at Philadelphia. Next to Magna Charta and the Declaration of Independence, the Declaration of

Principles then formulated, and signed by Whittier, is a document of which the generations unborn will be most proud. A copy of it framed in wood from Pennsylvania Hall, destroyed by a pro-slavery mob, was one of Whittier's most precious possessions.

In spite of his stand on an unpopular side, Whittier's character was appreciated by his fellow-citizens. He was elected a member of the Massachusetts State legislature in 1835. He held only one other public office — that of presidential elector. But the people of his own communion looked askance upon his political, reformatory, and literary achievements. He was even brought into danger of discipline, and it is said that in his later days he used to remark jokingly that not until he was old would the Quakers of his society show any willingness to put upon him the little dignities from which his position as a reformer had in his youth excluded him.

The very year that he was a member of the Massachusetts legislature, he had his first experience of a mob. George Thompson, the famous English abolitionist and member of Parliament, came to this country to preach abolition. It was noised abroad that he was brought over to disseminate dissension between North and South, so as to destroy American trade, to the advantage of British. This noble reformer had narrrowly escaped a mob in Salem. Whittier invited him to his East Haverhill home, that he might have perfect rest and quiet. The two men enjoyed making hay together and were entirely unmolested. At last they started to drive to Plymouth, N.H., to visit a prominent abolitionist there. On their way they stopped at Concord, where Thompson was invited to speak on reform.

After the lecture they found it impossible to leave the hall, which was surrounded by a mob of several hundred persons. On their way back, they were assailed with stones. Whittier declared that he understood how St. Paul felt when the Jews attacked him. Fortunately, their heads were not broken, but they were severely lamed. The mob surrounded the house and demanded that the Quaker and his guest should be handed over to them. His host opened the door and exclaimed: "Whoever comes in here must come in over my dead body." Decoyed away, the rabble returned with muskets and a cannon. Their lives were in danger. They managed to harness a horse, and then, when the gate was suddenly opened, they drove off at a furious gallop and escaped from the hooting mob, which one of themselves afterwards declared was like a throng of demons. At Plymouth they narrowly escaped another mobbing. Not long after, when Whittier was attending an extra session of the legislature, the female anti-slavery society meeting was broken up by a mob. The police rescued Garrison, just as they were going to hang him to a lamp-post. Whittier's sister was one of the delegates, and the two were stopping at the same house. Whittier managed to remove her to a place of safety; he and Samuel J. May sat up all night watching developments. Those were exciting times.

Most of the year Whittier, like Cincinnatus, worked his farm. His father had died, and the brunt of the burden of supporting the family rested on him. He was often seen in the fall of the year at the head of tide-water in the Merrimack, exchanging apples and vegetables for the salt-fish brought by coasting vessels. In the spring of March, 1838, he went to Philadelphia to edit the *Pennsylvania Freeman*, which had its offices in a large building built by the anti-slavery people, and named Pennsylvania Hall. It was publicly opened on the fifteenth of May with speeches, and a long poem by Whittier. That evening a stone was flung through one of the windows of the hall. This was the preliminary symptom of impending trouble. The next day a mob collected and disturbed the meetings with their jeers and yells. On the third day, in spite of the association's formal demand for protection, and the mayor's promise, the building was given into the hands of the mob, which sacked it and then set it on fire. The firemen refused to quench the flames and were complimented by the Southern press on their *noble conduct*. One paper printed a boasting letter from a participant saying: "Not a drop of water did they pour on that accursed Moloch until it was a heap of ruins."

A charitable shelter for colored orphans was also burned, and a colored church was attacked and wrecked. The members of the Pennsylvania Anti-slavery Society met the next morning after the outrage, beside the smoking ruins of their hall, and calmly elected their officers while a vast mob was still howling around them. Whittier's investment in the paper was lost, but he stayed in Philadelphia for about a year, when his failing health compelled him to return to Massachusetts. The East Haverhill farm was sold in 1840, and he removed with his mother, sister, and aunt to Amesbury, which was his *legal* residence through the rest of his life. Within ten or twelve minutes' walk of Whittier's house rises Pow-wow Hill, so often celebrated in his verse. The surrounding region which is visible from it has been well called his Ayrshire: far to the north the White Mountains are dimly visible, — his beloved Ossipee and Bearcamp. To the south, Agamenticus — Adamaticus, as the natives call it — stands in its purple isolation. The Isles of Shoals are visible, like rough stones in a turquoise arch, the lone line of beaches which he often called by name, and the rock-ribbed coast of Cape Ann. Scarcely a point which had not a legend, scarcely a legend which he did not put into verse.

After the death of his sister and the marriage of his niece, he resided during the most of the year with his cousins, at their beautiful country-seat at Oak Knoll, Danvers.

The storm and stress were past. Henceforth, for the most part, he devoted his genius to song. His watchword was : —

Our country, and Liberty and God for the Right.

He was not afraid to lift the whip of scorpion stings : he called the pro-slavery congressmen : —

> A passive herd of Northern mules,
>   Just braying from their purchased throats
> Whate'er their owner rules.

The Northern author of the congressional rule against receiving the petitions of the people in regard to slavery was thus held up to execration : —

> . . . the basest of the base,
>   The vilest of the vile, — . . .
>
> .   .   .   .
>
> A mark for every passing blast
> Of scorn to whistle through.

When he felt that Daniel Webster, whom he had so much admired, was recreant, he wrote against him that tremendous accusation entitled " Ichabod." He never ceased, however, to regret the severity of those awful lines, which make Browning's " Lost Leader " sound flat and insipid in comparison.

Whittier was never despondent. In the darkest hours he saw the rainbow promise bent on high.

He cried in 1844 to the men of Massachusetts : —

> Shrink not from strife unequal!
>   With the best is always hope;
> And ever in the sequel
>   God holds the right side up.

Thus, while he knew how to apply the lash, he also could cheer, and encourage, and advise. His practical common sense, his clear vision, saw far ahead.

It would be impossible to write the history of Emancipation and not recognize the influence of

Whittier's lyrics. Lacking in imagination, in grace, in what is commonly called poetic charm, often clumsy, ill-rhymed, and unrhythmical, they yet have an awakening power like that of a trumpet. Plain and unadorned, they appealed to a plain and simple people. They won their way by these very homely qualities.

Whittier learned from his parents the art of story-telling. Naturally, the Indians first appealed to him, and many of his earliest poems have the Red-skins as their heroes; speaking of "Mogg Megone" many years after it was written, he says : —

"Looking at it at the present time, it suggests the idea of a big Indian in his war-paint strutting about in Sir Walter Scott's plaid."

But the early history of New England was full of folk-lore, and Whittier had the ballad-maker's instinct. As he grew older, his sureness of touch increased. The homely names conferred on his native brooks and ponds fitted into his verse. Thus : —

> The dark pines sing on Ramoth Hill
> The slow song of the sea.

> The sweetbriar blooms on Kittery-side
> And green are Eliot's bowers.

And he talks about the "nuts of Wenham woods." One could quote hundreds of such felicitous touches, which endear a poet to his neighbors and then to his nation. Catching hold of the New England legends and turning them into homely

rhymes, as a ballad-singer would have done in
the early days, he becomes not only the poet, but
the creator of the legends. The very meaning of the
word "poet" is the maker. A friend sends him the
rough prose outline of a story connected with some
old house, and Whittier easily remodels it and
makes it his own. Thus he is the Poet of New
England, and as New England has colonized the
West, his fame spreads over the whole land. He
gets hearers for himself by this double capacity.
He is the ballad-maker; and in this view he stands
far higher as a poet than in his nobler but less
poetic capacity of Laureate of Freedom and Faith.
The word "Liberty" has a hundred rhymes; the
word "slave" its dozens. How the poet is put to it
when he wants to find a rhyme for "love"!
"Dove" and "above" and "glove" are about all
the words that are left to him. Whittier, with his
ease of rhyming, put little poetry but immense
feeling into his anti-slavery poems. Not by them
will he be judged as a poet.

He has still another claim on us. He was the
descendant of godly men and women. No American poet of his rank was so distinctively religious,
and yet his verse is absolutely

> undimmed
> By dust of theologic strife or breath
> Of sect, or cobwebs of scholastic lore.

He could not be kept within the narrow limits of a
sect. His religion was a vital principle with him.
Like his own "Quaker of the Olden Time," he made

his daily life a prayer. Faith in God was supreme. Read any of his hymns, his addresses to friends, his memorials to the dead; there are more than seventy of them gathered in the second volume of his collected works. How they speak of immortality and the Eternal Goodness! In one of his last poems, while he speaks almost mournfully of sitting alone and watching the

> warm, sweet day
> Lapse tenderly away,

he calms his troubled thought with these words : —

> Wait, while these few swift-passing days fulfil
> The wise disposing Will,
> And, in the evening as at morning, trust
> The All-merciful and Just.

> The solemn joy that soul communion feels
> Immortal life reveals;
> And human love, its prophecy and sign,
> Interprets love divine.

One of his last letters was written in favor of a union of the numerous sects in the one vital centre — the Christ. After this, it seems almost ungracious to speak critically of Whittier's work. He himself often wished that at least half of it were sunk in the Red Sea. A good deal of his early work had indeed

> The simple air and rustic dress
> And sign of haste and carelessness

which he attributes to it, but also it was

> More than the specious counterfeit
> Of sentiment or studied wit.

He calls his verse " simple lays of homely toil."

He may have written commonplaces, but he declared that he could *not* trace the *cold* and *heartless* commonplace.

Whittier was utterly color-blind; he also declared that he did not know anything of music, " not one tune from another." " The gods made him most unmusical," he whimsically remarked. Lack of musical ear is not uncommon in poets. Burns was behind all his schoolmates in that respect. Bryant had no music in his soul; Byron also lacked it. The rhythmic sense atones for the lack. Whittier, unlike Lowell, did not try to write in the Yankee dialect, but his origin betrayed itself. The long-suffering " r " was absolutely ignored. We have such rhymes as " gone — worn — horn "; " war — squaw "; " accurst — lust " (as though he pronounced it *accust*) ; " water — escort her "; " honor and scorner "; " off — serf "; " sisters — vistas "; " reward and God " (such infelicities did not offend his taste) ; " farmer — hammer "; " thus — curse "; " ever — leave her — Eva "; " favors — save us "; " tellers — Cinderellas "; " treasures — maize-ears "; " woody — sturdy "; " Katahdin's — gardens." He, like Byron (who pronounced " camelopard " " camel-leopard "), often put the wrong accents on words : " strong-*hold*," " *an*-cestral," " *pol*-troons," " grape-*vine*," " moon-*shine*," " romance," "*vio*lin" as though in two syllables. True to his Quaker origin, he rarely makes reference to music. Once he speaks of "The light viol and the mellow flute." He rarely indulges in comparisons. In that respect he is like the author of the Iliad. As a general thing his lines flow rather monotonously in the four-line ballad meter; he was neither bold nor very happy in more complicated structures of verse. His few sonnets were not successful. Sometimes he allowed the exigences of rhyme to force him into showing the Indian's birchen boat propelled by glancing oars. He once in a while wrote such lines as these : —

> The faded coloring of Time's tapestry
> Let Fancy with her dream-dipt brush supply.

Whittier, in conversation with his intimates, possessed a remarkable vein of humor; his letters are full of drolleries, but he seemed to have little sense of the ludicrous, else he could not have written such a line as

> Gurgled the waters of the moon-struck sea,

or

> From the rude board of Bonython
> Venison and succotash have gone.

He rarely indulged in alliteration, yet we find "greenly growing grain" and "Summer's shade and sunshine warm." In one place he boldly indulges for rhyme's sake in such bad grammar as this : —

> When Warkworth wood
> Closed o'er my steed and I.

And again: "twixt thou and I." In spite of these faults, we would not willingly let a line of Whittier's verse perish. Even the fugitive pieces of his youth, which he himself came to detest, the crudities of "Mogg Megone," are interesting and valuable. When his verse is studied chronologically, it is easy to see what constant progress he made. It was the noble growth of a New England pine, which, while the branches near the ground are dead and broken, still towers up higher and higher, with ever abundant foliage toward the sun-kissed top. And what pictures he painted!

Whittier, without the advantages, or so-called advantages, of college training, without ever travelling abroad, a hermit, almost, in his later years, keeping aloof from the people, painfully suffering from constant ill-health, unable to work half an hour at a time, ranks with the greatest of American men of letters. His prose is simple and pure; his verse goes right to the heart. It is free from the sentimentality and turbidity of Lowell, from the artificiality that we sometimes feel in Longfellow, from the classic coldness of Bryant. He was the poet of the people, and yet the cultured find no less to love and admire in him. To have written "Snow-Bound" alone would have been to achieve immortality. But Whittier wrote so many popular poems, which have become household words, that I have not even attempted to enumerate them or the date of their appearing.

He lived to see the crown of immortality unanimously conferred upon him. He lived to a grand old age, and yet he has said that for many years not merely the exertion of writing but even the mere thought of taking his pen into his hand brought on a terrible headache. Neither could he read with comfort. He therefore had to sit patiently and wait for Friend Death to come and lead him into that world where he believed the loved ones were waiting to welcome him. He died on the seventh of September, 1892, not at his favorite abiding-place at Oak Knoll, Danvers, but at Hampton Falls, N.H., where he was visiting the daughter of an old friend. Pure, simple, humble, unspoiled, full of love to God and man, triumphing in his faith, Whittier went forward into the unknown. Such a death is not to be deplored. He was willing, nay, anxious to go.

> Let the thick curtain fall;
> I better know than all
> How little I have gained,
> How vast the unattained.
>
> Sweeter than any sung
> My songs that found no tongue;
> Nobler than any fact
> My wish that failed of act.
>
> Others shall sing the song,
> Others shall right the wrong,
> Finish what I begin,
> And all I fail of, win!
>
> The airs of heaven blow o'er me,
> A glory shines before me
> Of what mankind shall be —
> Pure, generous, brave, and free.

Ring, bells in unreared steeples,
The joy of unborn peoples!
Sound, trumpets far off blown,
Your triumph is my own!

NATHAN HASKELL DOLE.

THE BRIDAL OF PENNACOOK.[1]

—•◆•—

WE had been wandering for many days
Through the rough northern country. We had seen
The sunset, with its bars of purple cloud,
Like a new heaven, shine upward from the lake
Of Winnepiseogee; and had felt
The sunrise breezes, midst the leafy aisles
Which stoop their summer beauty to the lips
Of the bright waters.   We had checked our steeds,

[1] Winnepurkit, otherwise called George, Sachem of Saugus, married a daughter of Passaconaway, the great Pennacook chieftain, in 1662. The wedding took place at Pennacook (now Concord, N. H.), and the ceremonies closed with a great feast. According to the usages of the chiefs, Passaconaway ordered a select number of his men to accompany the newly-married couple to the dwelling of the husband, where in turn there was another great feast. Some time after, the wife of Winnepurkit expressing a desire to visit her father's house, was permitted to go accompanied by a brave escort of her husband's chief men. But when she wished to return, her father sent a messenger to Saugus, informing her husband, and asking him to come and take her away. He returned for answer that he had escorted his wife to her father's house in a style that became a chief, and that now if she wished to return, her father must send her back in the same way. This Passaconaway refused to do, and it is said that here terminated the connection of his daughter with the Saugus chief. — *Vide Morton's New Canaan.*

Silent with wonder, where the mountain wall
Is piled to heaven; and, through the narrow rift
Of the vast rocks, against whose rugged feet
Beats the mad torrent with perpetual roar,
Where noonday is as twilight, and the wind
Comes burdened with the everlasting moan
Of forests and of far-off water-falls.
We had looked upward where the summer sky,
Tasselled with clouds light-woven by the sun,
Sprung its blue arch above the abutting crags
O'er-roofing the vast portal of the land
Beyond the wall of mountains.   We had passed
The high source of the Saco; and, bewildered
In the dwarf spruce-belts of the Crystal Hills,
Had heard above us, like a voice in the cloud,
The horn of Fabyan sounding; and atop
Of old Agioochook had seen the mountains
Piled to the northward, shagged with wood, and
        thick
As meadow mole hills — the far sea of Casco,
A white gleam on the horizon of the east;
Fair lakes, embosomed in the woods and hills;
Moosehillock's mountain range, and Kearsarge
Lifting his Titan forehead to the sun!

And we had rested underneath the oaks
Shadowing the bank, whose grassy spires are shaken
By the perpetual beating of the falls
Of the wild Ammonoosuc.   We had tracked
The winding Pemigewasset, overhung
By beechen shadows, whitening down its rocks,
Or lazily gliding through its intervals,

From waving rye-fields sending up the gleam
Of sunlit waters.   We had seen the moon
Rising behind Umbagog's eastern pines
Like a great Indian camp-fire; and its beams
At midnight spanning with a bridge of silver
The Merrimack by Uncanoonuc's falls.

There were five souls of us whom travel's chance
Had thrown together in these wild north hills : —
A city lawyer, for a month escaping
From his dull office, where the weary eye
Saw only hot brick walls and close thronged streets —
Briefless as yet, but with an eye to see
Life's sunniest side, and with a heart to take
Its chances all as God-sends ; and his brother,
Pale from long pulpit studies, yet retaining
The warmth and freshness of a genial heart,
Whose mirror of the beautiful and true,
In Man and Nature, was as yet undimmed
By dust of theologic strife, or breath
Of sect, or cobwebs of scholastic lore ;
Like a clear crystal calm of water, taking
The hue and image of o'erleaning flowers,
Sweet human faces, white clouds of the noon,
Slant starlight glimpses through the dewy leaves,
And tenderest moonrise.   'T was, in truth, a study,
To mark his spirit, alternating between
A decent and professional gravity
And an irreverent mirthfulness, which often
Laughed in the face of his divinity,
Plucked off the sacred ephod, quite unshrined
The oracle, and for the pattern priest

Left us the man.   A shrewd, sagacious merchant,
To whom the soiled sheet found in Crawford's inn,
Giving the latest news of city stocks
And sales of cotton had a deeper meaning
Than the great presence of the awful mountains
Glorified by the sunset ; — and his daughter,
A delicate flower on whom had blown too long
Those evil winds, which, sweeping from the ice
And winnowing the fogs of Labrador,
Shed their cold blight round Massachusetts' bay,
With the same breath which stirs Spring's opening
          leaves
And lifts her half-formed flower-bell on its stem,
Poisoning our sea-side atmosphere.

                              It chanced
That as we turned upon our homeward way,
A drear north-eastern storm came howling up
The valley of the Saco ; and that girl
Who had stood with us upon Mount Washington,
Her brown locks ruffled by the wind which whirled
In gusts around its sharp cold pinnacle,
Who had joined our gay trout-fishing in the streams
Which lave that giant's feet ; whose laugh was heard
Like a bird's carol on the sunrise breeze
Which swelled our sail amidst the lake's green
          islands,
Shrank from its harsh, chill breath, and visibly
          drooped
Like a flower in the frost.   So, in that quiet inn
Which looks from Conway on the mountains piled
Heavily against the horizon of the north,

Like summer thunder-clouds, we made our home:
And while the mist hung over dripping hills,
And the cold wind-driven rain-drops, all day long
Beat their sad music upon roof and pane,
We strove to cheer our gentle invalid.
The lawyer in the pauses of the storm
Went angling down the Saco, and, returning,
Recounted his adventures and mishaps;
Gave us the history of his scaly clients,
Mingling with ludicrous yet apt citations
Of barbarous law Latin, passages
From Izaak Walton's Angler, sweet and fresh
As the flower-skirted streams of Staffordshire
Where, under aged trees, the south-west wind
Of soft June mornings fanned the thin, white hair
Of the sage fisher.   And, if truth be told,
Our youthful candidate forsook his sermons,
His commentaries, articles and creeds
For the fair page of human loveliness —
The missal of young hearts, whose sacred text
Is music, its illumining sweet smiles.
He sang the songs she loved; and in his low,
Deep earnest voice, recited many a page
Of poetry — the holiest, tenderest lines
Of the sad bard of Olney — the sweet songs,
Simple and beautiful as Truth and Nature,
Of him whose whitened locks on Rydal Mount
Are lifted yet by morning breezes blowing
From the green hills, immortal in his lays.
And for myself, obedient to her wish,
I searched our landlord's proffered library:
A well-thumbed Bunyan, with its nice wood pictures

Of scaly fiends and angels not unlike them —
Watts' unmelodious psalms — Astrology's
Last home, a musty file of Almanacs,
And an old chronicle of border wars
And Indian history.   And, as I read
A story of the marriage of the Chief
Of Saugus to the dusky Weetamoo,
Daughter of Passaconaway, who dwelt
In the old time upon Merrimack,
Our fair one, in the playful exercise
Of her prerogative — the right divine
Of youth and beauty, — bade us versify
The legend, and with ready pencil sketched
Its plan and outlines, laughingly assigning
To each his part, and barring our excuses
With absolute will.   So, like the cavaliers
Whose voices still are heard in the Romance
Of silver-tongued Boccaccio, on the banks
Of Arno, with soft tales of love beguiling
The ear of languid beauty, plague-exiled
From stately Florence, we rehearsed our rhymes
To their fair auditor, and shared by turns
Her kind approval and her playful censure.

It may be that these fragments owe alone
To the fair setting of their circumstances —
The associations of time, scene and audience —
Their place amid the pictures which fill up
The chambers of my memory.   Yet I trust
That some, who sigh, while wandering in thought,
Pilgrims of Romance o'er the olden world,
That our broad land — our sea-like lakes, and moun-
     tains

Piled to the clouds, — our rivers overhung
By forests which have known no other change
For ages, than the budding and the fall
Of leaves — our valleys lovelier than those
Which the old poets sang of — should but figure
On the apocryphal chart of speculation
As pastures, wood-lots, mill-sites, with the privileges,
Rights and appurtenances, which make up
A Yankee Paradise — unsung, unknown,
To beautiful tradition; even their names,
Whose melody yet lingers like the last
Vibration of the red man's requiem,
Exchanged for syllables significant
Of cotton-mill and rail-car, — will look kindly
Upon this effort to call up the ghost
Of our dim Past, and listen with pleased ear
To the responses of the questioned Shade:

I. — THE MERRIMACK.

OH, child of that white-crested mountain whose
    springs
Gush forth in the shade of the cliff-eagle's wings,
Down whose slopes to the lowlands thy wild waters
    shine,
Leaping gray walls of rock, flashing through the
    dwarf pine.

From that cloud-curtained cradle so cold and so
    lone,
From the arms of that wintry-locked mother of
    stone,

By hills hung with forests, through vales wide and
    free,
Thy mountain-born brightness glanced down to the
    sea!

No bridge arched thy waters save that where the
    trees
Stretched their long arms above thee and kissed in
    the breeze :
No sound save the lapse of the waves on thy shores,
The plunging of otters, the light dip of oars.

Green-tufted, oak-shaded, by Amoskeag's fall
Thy twin Uncanoonucs rose stately and tall,
Thy Nashua meadows lay green and unshorn,
And the hills of Pentucket were tasselled with corn.

But thy Pennacook valley was fairer than these,
And greener its grasses and taller its trees,
Ere the sound of an axe in the forest had rung,
Or the mower his scythe in the meadows had swung.

In their sheltered repose looking out from the wood
The bark-builded wigwams of Pennacook stood,
There glided the corn-dance — the Council fire
    shone,
And against the red war-post the hatchet was thrown.

There the old smoked in silence their pipes, and the
    young
To the pike and the white perch their baited lines
    flung ;

There the boy shaped his arrows, and there the shy
    maid
Wove her many-hued baskets and bright wampum
    braid.

Oh, Stream of the Mountains! if answer of thine
Could rise from thy waters to question of mine,
Methinks through the din of thy thronged banks a
    moan
Of sorrow would swell for the days which have gone.

Not for thee the dull jar of the loom and the wheel,
The gliding of shuttles, the ringing of steel;
But that old voice of waters, of bird and of breeze,
The dip of the wild-fowl, the rustling of trees!

II. — THE BASHABA.[1]

LIFT we the twilight curtains of the Past,
    And turning from familiar sight and sound
Sadly and full of reverence let us cast
    A glance upon Tradition's shadowy ground,
Led by the few pale lights, which, glimmering round
    That dim, strange land of Eld, seem dying fast;

[1] This was the name which the Indians of New England
gave to two or three of their principal chiefs, to whom all their
inferior sagamores acknowledged allegiance. Passaconaway
seems to have been one of these chiefs. His residence was at
Pennacook. — *Mass. Hist. Coll.*, vol. iii., pp. 21, 22. " He was
regarded," says Hubbard, " as a great sorcerer, and his fame
was widely spread. It was said of him that he could cause a
green leaf to grow in winter, trees to dance, water to burn, etc.

And that which history gives not to the eye,
The faded coloring of Time's tapestry,
Let Fancy, with her dream-dipped brush supply.

Roof of bark and walls of pine,
Through whose chinks the sunbeams shine,
Tracing many a golden line
    On the ample floor within ;
Where upon that earth-floor stark,
Lay the gaudy mats of bark,
With the bear's hide, rough and dark,
    And the red-deer's skin.

Window-tracery, small and slight,
Woven of the willow white,
Lent a dimly-checkered light,
    And the night-stars glimmered down,
Where the lodge-fire's heavy smoke,
Slowly through an opening broke,
In the low roof, ribbed with oak,
    Sheathed with hemlock brown.

Gloomed behind the changeless shade,
By the solemn pine-wood made ;
Through the rugged palisade,
    In the open fore-ground planted,

He was, undoubtedly, one of those shrewd and powerful men
whose achievements are always regarded by a barbarous people
as the result of supernatural aid.   The Indians gave to such
the names of Powahs or Panisees."
    " The Panisees are men of great courage and wisdom, and
to these the Devill appeareth more familiarly than to others."
— *Winslow's Relation.*

Glimpses came of rowers rowing,
Stir of leaves and wild flowers blowing,
Steel-like gleams of water flowing,
    In the sun-light slanted.

Here the mighty Bashaba,
Held his long-unquestioned sway,
From the White Hills, far away,
    To the great sea's sounding shore
Chief of chiefs, his regal word
All the river Sachems heard,
At his call the war-dance stirred,
    Or was still once more.

There his spoils of chase and war,
Jaw of wolf and black bear's paw,
Panther's skin and eagle's claw,
    Lay beside his axe and bow ;
And, adown the roof-pole hung,
Loosely on a snake-skin strung,
In the smoke his scalp-locks swung
    Grimly to and fro.

Nightly down the river going,
Swifter was the hunter's rowing,
When he saw that lodge-fire glowing
    O'er the waters still and red ;
And the squaw's dark eye burned brighter,
And she drew her blanket tighter,
As, with quicker step and lighter,
    From that door she fled.

For that chief had magic skill,
And a Panisee's dark will,
Over powers of good and ill,
    Powers which bless and powers which ban —
Wizard lord of Pennacook,
Chiefs upon their war-path shook,
When they met the steady look
    Of that wise dark man.

Tales of him the gray squaw told,
When the winter night-wind cold
Pierced her blanket's thickest fold,
    And the fire burned low and small,
Till the very child a-bed,
Drew its bear-skin over head,
Shrinking from the pale lights shed
    On the trembling wall.

All the subtle spirits hiding
Under earth or wave, abiding
In the caverned rock, or riding
    Misty clouds or morning breeze;
Every dark intelligence,
Secret soul, and influence
Of all things which outward sense
    Feels, or hears or sees, —

These the wizard's skill confessed,
At his bidding banned or blessed,
Stormful woke or lulled to rest
    Wind and cloud, and fire and flood;

Burned for him the drifted snow,
Bade through ice fresh lilies blow,
And the leaves of summer grow
   Over winter's wood!

Not untrue that tale of old!
Now, as then, the wise and bold
All the powers of Nature hold
   Subject to their kingly will;
From the wondering crowds ashore,
Treading life's wild waters o'er,
As upon a marble floor,
   Moves the strong man still.

Still, to such, life's elements
With their sterner laws dispense,
And the chain of consequence
   Broken in their pathway lies;
Time and change their vassals making,
Flowers from icy pillows waking,
Tresses of the sunrise shaking
   Over midnight skies.

Still, to earnest souls, the sun
Rests on towered Gibeon,
And the moon of Ajalon
   Lights the battle-grounds of life;
To his aid the strong reverses,
Hidden powers and giant forces,
And the high stars in their courses
   Mingle in his strife!

III. — THE DAUGHTER.

THE soot-black brows of men — the yell
  Of women thronging round the bed —
The tinkling charm of ring and shell —
  The Powah whispering o'er the dead! —
All these the Sachem's home had known,
  When, on her journey long and wild
To the dim World of Souls, alone,
In her young beauty passed the mother of his child.

Three bow-shots from the Sachem's dwelling
  They laid her in the walnut shade,
Where a green hillock gently swelling
  Her fitting mound of burial made.
There trailed the vine in Summer hours —
  The tree-perched squirrel dropped his shell —
On velvet moss and pale-hued flowers,
Woven with leaf and spray, the softened sunshine
    fell!

The Indian's heart is hard and cold —
  It closes darkly o'er its care,
And, formed in Nature's sternest mould,
  Is slow to feel, and strong to bear.
The war-paint on the Sachem's face,
  Unwet with tears, shone fierce and red,
And, still in battle or in chase,
Dry leaf and snow-rime crisped beneath his foremost
    tread.

Yet, when her name was heard no more,
    And when the robe her mother gave,
And small, light moccasin she wore,
    Had slowly wasted on her grave,
Unmarked of him the dark maids sped
    Their sunset dance and moon-lit play;
No other shared his lonely bed,
No other fair young head upon his bosom lay.

A lone, stern man.   Yet, as sometimes
    The tempest-smitten tree receives
From one small root the sap which climbs
    Its topmost spray and crowning leaves,
So from his child the Sachem drew
    A life of Love and Hope, and felt
His cold and rugged nature through
The softness and the warmth of her young being
    melt.

A laugh which in the woodland rang
    Bemocking April's gladdest bird —
A light and graceful form which sprang
    To meet him when his step was heard —
Eyes by his lodge-fire flashing dark,
    Small fingers stringing bead and shell
Or weaving mats of bright-hued bark,—
With these the household-god [1] had graced his wig-
    wam well.

---

[1] "The Indians," says Roger Williams, "have a god whom
they call Wetuonanit, who presides over the household."

Child of the forest! — strong and free,
   Slight-robed, with loosely flowing hair,
She swam the lake or climbed the tree,
   Or struck the flying bird in air.
O'er the heaped drifts of Winter's moon
   Her snow-shoes tracked the hunter's way;
And dazzling in the Summer noon
The blade of her light oar threw off its shower of spray!

Unknown to her the rigid rule,
   The dull restraint, the chiding frown,
The weary torture of the school,
   The taming of wild nature down.
Her only lore, the legends told
   Around the hunter's fire at night;
Stars rose and set, and seasons rolled,
Flowers bloomed and snow-flakes fell, unquestioned
      in her sight.

Unknown to her the subtle skill
   With which the artist-eye can trace
In rock and tree and lake and hill
   The outlines of divinest grace;
Unknown the fine soul's keen unrest
   Which sees, admires, yet yearns alway;
Too closely on her mother's breast
To note her smiles of love the child of Nature lay!

It is enough for such to be
   Of common, natural things a part,
To feel with bird and stream and tree
   The pulses of the same great heart;

But we, from Nature long exiled
    In our cold homes of Art and Thought,
  Grieve like the stranger-tended child,
Which seeks its mother's arms, and sees but feels
      them not.

The garden rose may richly bloom
    In cultured soil and genial air,
To cloud the light of Fashion's room
    Or droop in Beauty's midnight hair;
In lonelier grace, to sun and dew
    The sweet-briar on the hill-side shows
Its single leaf and fainter hue,
Untrained and wildly free, yet still a sister rose!

Thus o'er the heart of Weetamoo
    Their mingling shades of joy and ill
The instincts of her nature threw, —
    The savage was a woman still.
Midst outlines dim of maiden schemes,
    Heart-colored prophecies of life,
Rose on the ground of her young dreams
The light of a new home — the lover and the wife!

IV. — THE WEDDING.

COOL and dark fell the Autumn night,
But the Bashaba's wigwam glowed with light,
For down from its roof by green withes hung
Flaring and smoking the pine-knots swung.

And along the river great wood fires
Shot into the night their long red spires,
Showing behind the tall, dark wood
Flashing before on the sweeping flood:

In the changeful wind, with shimmer and shade,
Now high, now low, that fire-light played,
On tree-leaves wet with evening dews,
On gliding water and still canoes.

The trapper that night on Turee's brook
And the weary fisher on Contoocook
Saw over the marshes and through the pine
And down on the river the dance-lights shine.

For the Saugus Sachem had come to woo
The Bashaba's daughter Weetamoo,
And laid at her father's feet that night
His softest furs and wampum white.

From the Crystal Hills to the far South East
The river Sagamores came to the feast;
And chiefs whose homes the sea-winds shook,
Sat down on the mats of Pennacook.

They came from Sunapee's shore of rock,
From the snowy sources of Snooganock,
And from rough Coös whose thick woods shake
Their pine-cones in Umbagog lake.

From Ammonoosuck's mountain pass
Wild as his home came Chepewass;

And the Keenomps of the hills which throw
Their shade on the Smile of Manito.

With pipes of peace and bows unstrung,
Glowing with paint came old and young,
In wampum and furs and feathers arrayed
To the dance and feast the Bashaba made.

Bird of the air and beast of the field,
All which the woods and waters yield
On dishes of birch and hemlock piled
Garnished and graced that banquet wild.

Steaks of the brown bear fat and large
From the rocky slopes of the Kearsarge;
Delicate trout from Babboosuck brook,
And salmon spear'd in the Contoocook;

Squirrels which fed where nuts fell thick
In the gravelly bed of the Otternic,
And small wild hens in reed-snares caught
From the banks of Sondagardee brought;

Pike and perch from the Suncook taken,
Nuts from the trees of the Black Hills shaken,
Cranberries picked in the Squamscot bog,
And grapes from the vines of Piscataquog:

And, drawn from that great stone vase which stands
In the river scooped by a spirit's hands,[1]

[1] There are rocks in the River at the Falls of Amoskeag, in the cavities of which, tradition says, the Indians formerly stored and concealed their corn.

Garnished with spoons of shell and horn,
Stood the birchen dishes of smoking corn.

Thus bird of the air and beast of the field,
All which the woods and the waters yield,
Furnished in that olden day
The bridal feast of the Bashaba.

And merrily when that feast was done
On the fire-lit green the dance begun,
With squaws' shrill stave, and deeper hum
Of old men beating the Indian drum.

Painted and plumed, with scalp locks flowing,
And red arms tossing and black eyes glowing,
Now in the light and now in the shade
Around the fires the dancers played.

The step was quicker, the song more shrill,
And the beat of the small drums louder still
Whenever within the circle drew
The Saugus Sachem and Weetamoo.

The moons of forty winters had shed
Their snow upon that chieftain's head,
And toil and care, and battle's chance
Had seamed his hard dark countenance.

A fawn beside the bison grim —
Why turns the bride's fond eye on him,
In whose cold look is naught beside
The triumph of a sullen pride?

Ask why the graceful grape entwines
The rough oak with her arm of vines;
And why the gray rock's rugged cheek
The soft lips of the mosses seek:

Why, with wise instinct, Nature seems
To harmonize her wide extremes,
Linking the stronger with the weak,
The haughty with the soft and meek!

V. — THE NEW HOME.

A WILD and broken landscape, spiked with firs,
   Roughening the bleak horizon's northern edge,
Steep, cavernous hill-side, where black hemlock spurs
   And sharp, gray splinters of the wind-swept ledge
Pierced the thin-glaz'd ice, or bristling rose,
Where the cold rim of the sky sunk down upon the
     snows.

And eastward cold, wide marshes stretched away,
   Dull, dreary flats without a bush or tree,
O'er-crossed by icy creeks, where twice a day
   Gurgled the waters of the moon-struck sea;
And faint with distance came the stifled roar,
The melancholy lapse of waves on that low shore.

No cheerful village with its mingling smokes,
   No laugh of children wrestling in the snow,
No camp-fire blazing through the hill-side oaks,
   No fishers kneeling on the ice below;

Yet midst all desolate things of sound and view,
Through the long winter moons smiled dark-eyed
    Weetamoo.

Her heart had found a home; and freshly all
   Its beautiful affections overgrew
Their rugged prop.   As o'er some granite wall
   Soft vine leaves open to the moistening dew
And warm bright sun, the love of that young wife
Found on a hard cold breast the dew and warmth of
    life.

The steep bleak hills, the melancholy shore,
   The long dead level of the marsh between,
A coloring of unreal beauty wore
   Through the soft golden mist of young love seen,
For o'er those hills and from that dreary plain,
Nightly she welcomed home her hunter chief again.

No warmth of heart, no passionate burst of feeling
   Repaid her welcoming smile, and parting kiss,
No fond and playful dalliance half concealing,
   Under the guise of mirth, its tenderness;
But, in their stead, the warrior's settled pride,
And vanity's pleased smile with homage satisfied.

Enough for Weetamoo, that she alone
   Sat on his mat and slumbered at his side;
That he whose fame to her young ear had flown,
   Now looked upon her proudly as his bride;
That he whose name the Mohawk trembling heard
Vouchsafed to her at times a kindly look or word.

For she had learned the maxims of her race,
    Which teach the woman to become a slave
And feel herself the pardonless disgrace
    Of love's fond weakness in the wise and brave —
The scandal and the shame which they incur,
Who give to woman all which man requires of her.

So passed the winter moons.   The sun at last
    Broke link by link the frost chain of the rills,
And the warm breathings of the southwest passed
    Over the hoar rime of the Saugus hills,
The gray and desolate marsh grew green once more,
And the birch-tree's tremulous shade fell round the
        Sachem's door.

Then from far Pennacook swift runners came,
    With gift and greeting for the Saugus chief;
Beseeching him in the great Sachem's name,
    That, with the coming of the flower and leaf,
The song of birds, the warm breeze and the rain,
Young Weetamoo might greet her lonely sire again.

And Winnepurkit called his chiefs together,
    And a grave council in his wigwam met,
Solemn and brief in words, considering whether
    The rigid rules of forest etiquette
Permitted Weetamoo once more to look
Upon her father's face and green-banked Pennacook.

With interludes of pipe-smoke and strong water,
    The forest sages pondered, and at length,

Concluded in a body to escort her
  Up to her father's home of pride and strength,
Impressing thus on Pennacook a sense
Of Winnepurkit's power and regal consequence.

So through old woods which Aukeetamit's [1] hand
  A soft and many-shaded greenness lent,
Over high breezy hills, and meadow land
  Yellow with flowers, the wild procession went,
Till rolling down its wooded banks between,
A broad, clear, mountain stream, the Merrimack was
      seen.

The hunter leaning on his bow undrawn —
  The fisher lounging on the pebbled shores,
Squaws in the clearing dropping the seed-corn,
  Young children peering through the wigwam doors,
Saw with delight, surrounded by her train
Of painted Saugus braves, their Weetamoo again.

VI. — AT PENNACOOK.

THE hills are dearest which our childish feet
Have climbed the earliest; and the streams most
      sweet,
Are ever those at which our young lips drank,
Stooped to their waters o'er the grassy bank:

Midst the cold dreary sea-watch, Home's hearth-light
Shines round the helmsman plunging through the
      night;

---

[1] The Spring God. — See Roger Williams's *Key,* etc.

And still, with inward eye, the traveller sees
In close, dark, stranger streets his native trees.

The home-sick dreamer's brow is nightly fanned
By breezes whispering of his native land,
And, on the stranger's dim and dying eye,
The soft, sweet pictures of his childhood lie!

Joy then for Weetamoo, to sit once more
A child upon her father's wigwam floor!
Once more with her old fondness to beguile
From his cold eye the strange light of a smile.

The long bright days of Summer swiftly passed,
The dry leaves whirled in Autumn's rising blast,
And evening cloud and whitening sunrise rime
Told of the coming of the winter time.

But vainly looked, the while, young Weetamoo,
Down the dark river for her chief's canoe;
No dusky messenger from Saugus brought
The grateful tidings which the young wife sought.

At length a runner, from her father sent
To Winnepurkit's sea-cooled wigwam went:
"Eagle of Saugus, — in the woods the dove
Mourns for the shelter of thy wings of love."

But the dark chief of Saugus turned aside
In the grim anger of hard-hearted pride;
"I bore her as became a chieftain's daughter,
Up to her home beside the gliding water.

"If now no more a mat for her is found
Of all which line her father's wigwam round,
Let Pennacook call out his warrior train
And send her back with wampum gifts again."

The baffled runner turned upon his track,
Bearing the words of Winnepurkit back.
"Dog of the Marsh," cried Pennacook, "no more
Shall child of mine sit on his wigwam floor.

"Go — let him seek some meaner squaw to spread
The stolen bear-skin of his beggar's bed:
Son of a fish-hawk! — let him dig his clams
For some vile daughter of the Agawams,

"Or coward Nipmucks! — may his scalp dry black
In Mohawk smoke, before I send her back."
He shook his clenched hand towards the ocean wave
While hoarse assent his listening council gave.

Alas poor bride! — can thy grim sire impart
His iron hardness to thy woman's heart?
Or cold self-torturing pride like his atone
For love denied and life's warm beauty flown?

On Autumn's gray and mournful grave the snow
Hung its white wreaths; with stifled voice and low
The river crept, by one vast bridge o'ercrossed,
Built by the hoar-locked artisan of Frost.

And many a Moon in beauty newly born
Pierced the red sunset with her silver horn,

Or, from the east across her azure field,
Rolled the wide brightness of her full-orbed shield.

Yet Winnepurkit came not — on the mat
Of the scorned wife her dusky rival sat,
And he, the while, in Western woods afar —
Urged the long chase, or trod the path of war.

Dry up thy tears, young daughter of a chief!
Waste not on him the sacredness of grief;
Be the fierce spirit of thy sire thine own,
His lips of scorning, and his heart of stone.

What heeds the warrior of a hundred fights,
The storm-worn watcher through long hunting nights,
Cold, crafty, proud, of woman's weak distress,
Her home-bound grief and pining loneliness?

VII. — THE DEPARTURE.

THE wild March rains had fallen fast and long
The snowy mountains of the North among,
Making each vale a water-course — each hill
Bright with the cascade of some new-made rill.

Gnawed by the sunbeams, softened by the rain,
Heaved underneath by the swollen current's strain,
The ice-bridge yielded, and the Merrimack
Bore the huge ruin crashing down its track.

On that strong turbid water, a small boat
Guided by one weak hand was seen to float,
Evil the fate which loosed it from the shore,
Too early voyager with too frail an oar !

Down the vexed centre of that rushing tide,
The thick huge ice-blocks threatening either side,
The foam-white rocks of Amoskeag in view,
With arrowy swiftness sped that light canoe.

The trapper, moistening his moose's meat
On the wet bank by Uncanoonuc's feet,
Saw the swift boat flash down the troubled stream —
Slept he, or waked he ? — was it truth or dream ?

The straining eye bent fearfully before,
The small hand clenching on the useless oar,
The bead-wrought blanket trailing o'er the water —
He knew them all — wo for the Sachem's daughter!

Sick and aweary of her lonely life,
Heedless of peril the still faithful wife
Had left her mother's grave, her father's door,
To seek the wigwam of her chief once more.

Down the white rapids like a sear leaf whirled,
On the sharp rocks and piled up ices hurled,
Empty and broken, circled the canoe
In the vexed pool below — but, where was Weetamoo?

VIII. — SONG OF INDIAN WOMEN.

THE Dark eye has left us,
  The Spring-bird has flown,
On the pathway of spirits
  She wanders alone.
The song of the wood-dove has died on our shore
Mat wonck kunna-monee! [1] — We hear it no more!

Oh, dark water Spirit!
  We cast on thy wave
These furs which may never
  Hang over her grave;
Bear down to the lost one the robes that she wore;
Mat wonck kunna-monee! — We see her no more!

Of the strange land she walks in
  No Powah has told:
It may burn with the sunshine,
  Or freeze with the cold.
Let us give to our lost one the robes that she wore,
Mat wonck kunna-monee! — We see her no more!

The path she is treading
  Shall soon be our own;
Each gliding in shadow
  Unseen and alone! —
In vain shall we call on the souls gone before —
Mat wonck kunna-monee! — They hear us no more!

---

[1] "Mat wonck kunna-monee." We shall see thee or her
no more. — *Vide* Roger Williams's *Key to the Indian Language.*

Oh mighty Sowanna ! [1]
　　Thy gateways unfold,
　From the wigwam of sunset
　　Lift curtains of gold !
Take home the poor Spirit whose journey is o'er —
Mat wonck kunna monee ! — We see her no more !

So sang the Children of the Leaves beside
The broad, dark river's coldly-flowing tide,
Now low, now harsh, with sob-like pause and swell
On the high wind their voices rose and fell.
Nature's wild music — sounds of wind-swept trees,
The scream of birds, the wailing of the breeze,
The roar of waters, steady, deep and strong,
Mingled and murmured in that farewell song.

[1] " The Great South West God." — See Roger Williams's *Observations*, etc.

LEGENDARY.

THE MERRIMACK.

["The Indians speak of a beautiful river, far to the South,
which they call Merrimack." — SIEUR DE MONTS, 1604.]

STREAM of my fathers! sweetly still
The sunset rays thy valley fill;
Poured slantwise down the long defile,
Wave, wood, and spire beneath them smile.
I see the winding Powow fold
The green hill in its belt of gold,
And following down its wavy line,
Its sparkling waters blend with thine.
There's not a tree upon thy side,
Nor rock, which thy returning tide
As yet hath left abrupt and stark
Above thy evening water-mark;
No calm cove with its rocky hem,
No isle whose emerald swells begem
Thy broad, smooth current; not a sail
Bowed to the freshening ocean gale;
No small boat with its busy oars,
Nor gray wall sloping to thy shores;
Nor farm-house with its maple shade,
Or rigid poplar colonnade,

But lies distinct and full in sight,
Beneath this gush of sunset light.
Centuries ago, that harbor-bar,
Stretching its length of foam afar,
And Salisbury's beach of shining sand,
And yonder island's wave-smoothed strand,
Saw the adventurer's tiny sail
Flit, stooping from the eastern gale ; [1]
And o'er these woods and waters broke
The cheer from Britain's hearts of oak,
As brightly on the voyager's eye,
Weary of forest, sea, and sky,
Breaking the dull continuous wood,
The Merrimack rolled down his flood ;
Mingling that clear pellucid brook,
Which channels vast Agioochook
When spring-time's sun and shower unlock
The frozen fountains of the rock,
And more abundant waters given
From that pure lake, " The Smile of Heaven," [2]
Tributes from vale and mountain side —
With ocean's dark, eternal tide!

On yonder rocky cape, which braves
The stormy challenge of the waves,
Midst tangled vine and dwarfish wood,
The hardy Anglo-Saxon stood,

[1] The celebrated Captain Smith, after resigning the government of the colony in Virginia, in his capacity of " Admiral of New England," made a careful survey of the coast from Penobscot to Cape Cod, in the summer of 1614.

[2] Lake Winnipiseogee — *The Smile of the Great Spirit* — the source of one of the branches of the Merrimack.

Planting upon the topmost crag
The staff of England's battle-flag;
And, while from out its heavy fold
Saint George's crimson cross unrolled,
Midst roll of drum and trumpet blare,
And weapons brandishing in air,
He gave to that lone promontory
The sweetest name in all his story; [1]
Of her, the flower of Islam's daughters,
Whose harems look on Stamboul's waters —
Who, when the chance of war had bound
The Moslem chain his limbs around,
Wreathed o'er with silk that iron chain,
Soothed with her smiles his hours of pain,
And fondly to her youthful slave
A dearer gift than freedom gave.

But look! — the yellow light no more
Streams down on wave and verdant shore;
And clearly on the calm air swells
The twilight voice of distant bells.
From Ocean's bosom, white and thin
The mists come slowly rolling in;
Hills, woods, the river's rocky rim,
Amidst the sea-like vapor swim,
While yonder lonely coast-light set
Within its wave-washed minaret,

---

[1] Captain Smith gave to the promontory, now called Cape
Ann, the name of Tragabizanda, in memory of his young and
beautiful mistress of that name, who, while he was a captive at
Constantinople, like Desdemona, "loved him for the dangers
he had passed."

Half quenched, a beamless star and pale,
Shines dimly through its cloudy veil!

Home of my fathers! — I have stood
Where Hudson rolled his lordly flood:
Seen sunrise rest and sunset fade
Along his frowning Palisade;
Looked down the Appalachian peak
On Juniata's silver streak;
Have seen along his valley gleam
The Mohawk's softly winding stream;
The level light of sunset shine
Through broad Potomac's hem of pine;
And autumn's rainbow-tinted banner
Hang lightly o'er the Susquehanna;
Yet, wheresoe'er his step might be,
Thy wandering child looked back to thee!
Heard in his dreams thy river's sound
Of murmuring on its pebbly bound,
The unforgotten swell and roar
Of waves on thy familiar shore;
And saw, amidst the curtained gloom
And quiet of his lonely room,
Thy sunset scenes before him pass;
As, in Agrippa's magic glass,
The loved and lost arose to view,
Remembered groves in greenness grew,
Bathed still in childhood's morning dew,
Along whose bowers of beauty swept
Whatever Memory's mourners wept,
Sweet faces, which the charnel kept,
Young, gentle eyes, which long had slept;

And while the gazer leaned to trace,
More near, some dear familiar face,
He wept to find the vision flown —
A phantom and a dream alone !

THE NORSEMEN.

[Some three or four years since, a fragment of a statue, rudely chiselled from dark gray stone, was found in the town of Brad-ford, on the Merrimack. Its origin must be left entirely to conjecture. The fact that the ancient Northmen visited New England, some centuries before the discoveries of Columbus, is now very generally admitted.]

GIFT from the cold and silent Past !
A relic to the present cast ;
Left on the ever-changing strand
Of shifting and unstable sand,
Which wastes beneath the steady chime
And beating of the waves of Time !
Who from its bed of primal rock
First wrenched thy dark, unshapely block ?
Whose hand, of curious skill untaught,
Thy rude and savage outline wrought ?

The waters of my native stream
Are glancing in the sun's warm beam :
From sail-urged keel and flashing oar
The circles widen to its shore ;
And cultured field and peopled town
Slope to its willowed margin down.

Yet, while this morning breeze is bringing
The mellow sound of church-bells ringing,
And rolling wheel, and rapid jar
Of the fire-winged and steedless car,
And voices from the wayside near
Come quick and blended on my ear,
A spell is in this old gray stone —
My thoughts are with the Past alone !
A change ! — The steepled town no more
Stretches along the sail-thronged shore ;
Like palace-domes in sunset's cloud,
Fade sun-gilt spire and mansion proud !
Spectrally rising where they stood,
I see the old, primeval wood :
Dark, shadow-like, on either hand
I see its solemn waste expand :
It climbs the green and cultured hill,
It arches o'er the valley's rill ;
And leans from cliff and crag, to throw
Its wild arms o'er the stream below.
Unchanged, alone, the same bright river
Flows on, as it will flow forever !
I listen, and I hear the low
Soft ripple where its waters go ;
I hear behind the panther's cry,
The wild bird's scream goes thrilling by,
And shyly on the river's brink
The deer is stooping down to drink.

But hark ! — from wood and rock flung back,
What sound comes up the Merrimack ?
What sea-worn barks are those which throw

The light spray from each rushing prow?
Have they not in the North Sea's blast
Bowed to the waves the straining mast?
Their frozen sails the low, pale sun
Of Thulè's night has shone upon ;
Flapped by the sea-wind's gusty sweep
Round icy drift, and headland steep.
Wild Jutland's wives and Lochlin's daughters
Have watched them fading o'er the waters,
Lessening through driving mist and spray,
Like white-winged sea-birds on their way!
Onward they glide — and now I view
Their iron-armed and stalwart crew ;
Joy glistens in each wild blue eye,
Turned to green earth and summer sky :
Each broad, seamed breast has cast aside
Its cumbering vest of shaggy hide ;
Bared to the sun and soft warm air,
Streams back the Norsemen's yellow hair.
I see the gleam of axe and spear,
The sound of smitten shields I hear,
Keeping a harsh and fitting time
To Saga's chant, and Runic rhyme ;
Such lays as Zetland's Skald has sung,
His gray and naked isles among ;
Or muttered low at midnight hour
Round Odin's mossy stone of power.
The wolf beneath the Arctic moon
Has answered to that startling rune ;
The Gaal has heard its stormy swell,
The light Frank knows its summons well ;
Iona's sable-stoled Culdee

Has heard it sounding o'er the sea,
And swept with hoary beard and hair
His altar's foot in trembling prayer!

'Tis past — the 'wildering vision dies
In darkness on my dreaming eyes!
The forest vanishes in air —
Hill-slope and vale lie starkly bare;
I hear the common tread of men,
And hum of work-day life again:
The mystic relic seems alone
A broken mass of common stone;
And if it be the chiselled limb
Of Berserkar or idol grim —
A fragment of Valhalla's Thor,
The stormy Viking's god of War,
Of Praga of the Runic lay,
Or love awakening Siona,
I know not — for no graven line,
Nor Druid mark, nor Runic sign,
Is left me here, by which to trace
Its name, or origin, or place.

Yet, for this vision of the Past,
This glance upon its darkness cast,
My spirit bows in gratitude
Before the Giver of all good,
Who fashioned so the human mind,
That, from the waste of Time behind
A simple stone, or mound of earth,
Can summon the departed forth;

Quicken the Past to life again —
The Present lose in what hath been,
And in their primal freshness show
The buried forms of long ago.
As if a portion of that Thought
By which the Eternal will is wrought,
Whose impulse fills anew with breath
The frozen solitude of Death,
To mortal mind were sometimes lent,
To mortal musings sometimes sent,
To whisper — even when it seems
But Memory's phantasy of dreams --
Through the mind's waste of woe and sin,
Of an immortal origin!

1841.

CASSANDRA SOUTHWICK.

[In the following ballad, the author has endeavored to display the strong enthusiasm of the early Quaker, the short-sighted intolerance of the clergy and magistrates, and that sympathy with the oppressed, which the "common people," when not directly under the control of spiritual despotism, have ever evinced. He is not blind to the extravagance of language and action which characterized some of the pioneers of Quakerism in New England, and which furnished persecution with its solitary but most inadequate excuse.

The ballad has its foundation upon a somewhat remarkable event in the history of Puritan intolerance. Two young persons, son and daughter of Lawrence Southwick, of Salem, who had himself been imprisoned and deprived of all his property for having entertained two Quakers at his house, were fined

ten pounds each for non-attendance at church, which they were
unable to pay. The case being represented to the General
Court, at Boston, that body issued an order, which may still be
seen on the court records, bearing the signature of Edward
Rawson, Secretary, by which the treasurer of the County was
"fully empowered to *sell the said persons* to any of the English
nation at *Virginia or Barbadoes*, to answer said fines." An
attempt was made to carry this barbarous order into execution,
but no shipmaster was found willing to convey them to the
West Indies. — *Vide* Sewall's *History*, pp. 225, 226, G. Bishop.]

To the God of all sure mercies let my blessing rise
　　　to-day,
From the scoffer and the cruel He hath plucked the
　　　spoil away, —
Yea, He who cooled the furnace around the faithful
　　　three,
And tamed the Chaldean lions, hath set His hand-
　　　maid free!

Last night I saw the sunset melt through my prison
　　　bars,
Last night across my damp earth-floor fell the pale
　　　gleam of stars ;
In the coldness and the darkness all through the
　　　long night time,
My grated casement whitened with Autumn's early
　　　rime.

Alone, in that dark sorrow, hour after hour crept
　　　by ;
Star after star looked palely in and sank adown the
　　　sky ;

No sound amid night's stillness, save that which
    seemed to be
The dull and heavy beating of the pulses of the sea;

All night I sat unsleeping, for I knew that on the
    morrow
The ruler and the cruel priest would mock me in my
    sorrow,
Dragged to their place of market, and bargained for
    and sold,
Like a lamb before the shambles, like a heifer from
    the fold !

Oh, the weakness of the flesh was there — the
    shrinking and the shame;
And the low voice of the Tempter like whispers to
    me came:
"Why sit'st thou thus forlornly !" the wicked mur-
    mur said,
"Damp walls thy bower of beauty, cold earth thy
    maiden bed?

"Where be the smiling faces, and voices soft and
    sweet,
Seen in thy father's dwelling, heard in the pleasant
    street?
Where be the youths, whose glances the summer
    Sabbath through
Turned tenderly and timidly unto thy father's pew ?

"Why sit'st thou here, Cassandra? — Bethink thee
    with what mirth

Thy happy schoolmates gather around the warm
　　　bright hearth ;
How the crimson shadows tremble on foreheads
　　　white and fair,
On eyes of merry girlhood, half hid in golden hair.

" Not for thee the hearth-fire brightens, not for thee
　　　kind words are spoken,
Not for thee the nuts of Wenham woods by laughing
　　　boys are broken,
No first-fruits of the orchard within thy lap are
　　　laid,
For thee no flowers of Autumn the youthful hunters
　　　braid.

" Oh ! weak, deluded maiden ! — by crazy fancies
　　　led,
With wild and raving railers an evil path to
　　　tread ;
To leave a wholesome worship, and teaching pure
　　　and sound ;
And mate with maniac women, loose-haired and sack-
　　　cloth-bound.

" Mad scoffers of the priesthood, who mock at things
　　　divine,
Who rail against the pulpit, and holy bread and
　　　wine ;
Sore from their cart-tail scourgings, and from the
　　　pillory lame,
Rejoicing in their wretchedness, and glorying in
　　　their shame.

"And what a fate awaits thee?—a sadly toiling
   slave,
Dragging the slowly lengthening chain of bondage
      to the grave!
Think of thy woman's nature, subdued in hopeless
      thrall,
The easy prey of any, the scoff and scorn of all!"

Oh!—ever as the Tempter spoke, and feeble
      Nature's fears
Wrung drop by drop the scalding flow of unavailing
      tears,
I wrestled down the evil thoughts, and strove in
      silent prayer,
To feel, oh, Helper of the weak!—that Thou indeed
      wert there!

I thought of Paul and Silas, within Philippi's cell,
And how from Peter's sleeping limbs the prison-
      shackles fell,
Till I seemed to hear the trailing of an angel's robe
      of white,
And to feel a blessed presence invisible to sight.

Bless the Lord for all His mercies!—for the peace
      and love I felt,
Like dew of Hermon's holy hill, upon my spirit
      melt;
When, "Get behind me, Satan!" was the language
      of my heart,
And I felt the Evil Tempter with all his doubts
      depart.

Slow broke the gray cold morning; again the sun-
　　shine fell,
Flecked with the shade of bar and grate within my
　　lonely cell;
The hoar frost melted on the wall, and upward from
　　the street
Came careless laugh and idle word, and tread of
　　passing feet.

At length the heavy bolts fell back, my door was
　　open cast,
And slowly at the sheriff's side, up the long street
　　I passed;
I heard the murmur round me, and felt, but dared
　　not see,
How, from every door and window, the people gazed
　　on me.

And doubt and fear fell on me, shame burned upon
　　my cheek,
Swam earth and sky around me, my trembling limbs
　　grew weak:
" Oh, Lord! support thy handmaid; and from her
　　soul cast out
The fear of man, which brings a snare — the weak-
　　ness and the doubt."

Then the dreary shadows scattered like a cloud in
　　morning's breeze,
And a low deep voice within me seemed whispering
　　words like these:

" Though thy earth be as the iron, and thy heaven
    a brazen wall,
Trust still His loving kindness whose power is
    over all."

We paused at length, where at my feet the sunlit
    waters broke
On glaring reach of shining beach, and shingly wall
    of rock ;
The merchant-ships lay idly there, in hard clear
    lines on high,
Tracing with rope and slender spar their net-work
    on the sky.

And there were ancient citizens, cloak-wrapped and
    grave and cold,
And grim and stout sea-captains with faces bronzed
    and old,
And on his horse, with Rawson, his cruel clerk at
    hand,
Sat dark and haughty Endicott, the ruler of the
    land.

And poisoning with his evil words the ruler's ready
    ear,
The priest leaned o'er his saddle, with laugh and
    scoff and jeer ;
It stirred my soul, and from my lips the seal of
    silence broke,
As if through woman's weakness a warning spirit
    spoke.

I cried, "The Lord rebuke thee, thou smiter of the
    meek,
Thou robber of the righteous, thou trampler of the
    weak !
Go light the dark, cold hearth-stones — go turn the
    prison lock
Of the poor hearts thou hast hunted, thou wolf amid
    the flock ! "

Dark lowered the brows of Endicott, and with a
    deeper red
O'er Rawson's wine-empurpled cheek the flush of
    anger spread ;
"Good people," quoth the white-lipped priest, "heed
    not her words so wild,
Her Master speaks within her — the Devil owns his
    child ! "

But gray heads shook, and young brows knit, the
    while the sheriff read
That law the wicked rulers against the poor have
    made,
Who to their house of Rimmon and idol priesthood
    bring
No bended knee of worship, nor gainful offering.

Then to the stout sea-captains the sheriff turning
    said :
"Which of ye, worthy seamen, will take this Quaker
    maid?
In the Isle of fair Barbadoes, or on Virginia's shore,
You may hold her at a higher price than Indian girl
    or Moor."

Grim and silent stood the captains; and when again
    he cried,
"Speak out, my worthy seamen!"—no voice, no
    sign replied;
But I felt a hard hand press my own, and kind words
    met my ear:
"God bless thee, and preserve thee, my gentle girl
    and dear!"

A weight seemed lifted from my heart, a pitying
    friend was nigh,
I felt it in his hard, rough hand, and saw it in his
    eye;
And when again the sheriff spoke, that voice, so kind
    to me,
Growled back its stormy answer like the roaring of
    the sea:

"Pile my ship with bars of silver—pack with coins
    of Spanish gold,
From keel-piece up to deck-plank, the roomage of her
    hold,
By the living God who made me!—I would sooner
    in your bay
Sink ship and crew and cargo, than bear this child
    away!"

"Well answered, worthy captain, shame on their
    cruel laws!"
Ran through the crowd in murmurs loud the people's
    just applause.

" Like the herdsmen of Tekoa, in Israel of old,
Shall we see the poor and righteous again for silver
    sold ? "

I looked on haughty Endicott; with weapon half
    way drawn,
Swept round the throng his lion glare of bitter hate
    and scorn;
Fiercely he drew his bridle rein, and turned in silence
    back,
And sneering priest and baffled clerk rode murmur-
    ing in his track.

Hard after them the sheriff looked, in bitterness of
    soul;
Thrice smote his staff upon the ground, and crushed
    his parchment roll.
"Good friends," he said, "since both have fled, the
    ruler and the priest,
Judge ye, if from their further work I be not well
    released."

Loud was the cheer which, full and clear, swept round
    the silent bay,
As, with kind words and kinder looks, he bade me
    go my way;
For He who turns the courses of the streamlet of
    the glen,
And the river of great waters, had turned the hearts
    of men.

Oh, at that hour the very earth seemed changed
     beneath my eye,
A holier wonder round me rose the blue walls of
     the sky,
A lovelier light on rock and hill, and stream and
     woodland lay,
And softer lapsed on sunnier sands the waters of the
     bay.

Thanksgiving to the Lord of life ! — to Him all
     praises be,
Who from the hands of evil men hath set His hand-
     maid free ;
All praise to Him before whose power the mighty
     are afraid,
Who takes the crafty in the snare, which for the
     poor is laid !

Sing, oh, my soul, rejoicingly, on evening's twilight
     calm
Uplift the loud thanksgiving — pour forth the grate-
     ful psalm ;
Let all dear hearts with me rejoice, as did the saints
     of old,
When of the Lord's good angel the rescued Peter
     told.

And weep and howl, ye evil priests and mighty men
     of wrong,
The Lord shall smite the proud and lay His hand
     upon the strong.

Woe to the wicked rulers in His avenging hour!
Woe to the wolves who seek the flocks to raven and
    devour:

But let the humble ones arise, — the poor in heart be
    glad,
And let the mourning ones again with robes of praise
    be clad,
For He who cooled the furnace, and smoothed the
    stormy wave,
And tamed the Chaldean lions, is mighty still to save!

    1842.

FUNERAL TREE OF THE SOKOKIS.[1]

AROUND Sebago's lonely lake
There lingers not a breeze to break
The mirror which its waters make.

The solemn pines along its shore,
The firs which hang its gray rocks o'er,
Are painted on its glassy floor.

[1] Polan, a chief of the Sokokis Indians, the original inhabitants of the country lying between Agamenticus and Casco Bay, was killed in a skirmish at Windham, on the Sebago lake, in the spring of 1756. He claimed all the lands on both sides of the Presumpscot River to its mouth at Casco, as his own. He was shrewd, subtle, and brave. After the white men had retired, the surviving Indians "swayed" or bent down a young tree until its roots were turned up, placed the body of their chief beneath them, and then released the tree to spring back to its former position.

The sun looks o'er, with hazy eye,
The snowy mountain-tops which lie
Piled coldly up against the sky.

Dazzling and white! save where the bleak,
Wild winds have bared some splintering peak,
Or snow-slide left its dusky streak.

Yet green are Saco's banks below,
And belts of spruce and cedar show,
Dark fringing round those cones of snow.

The earth hath felt the breath of spring,
Though yet on her deliverer's wing
The lingering frosts of winter cling.

Fresh grasses fringe the meadow-brooks,
And mildly from its sunny nooks
The blue eye of the violet looks.

And odors from the springing grass,
The sweet birch and the sassafras,
Upon the scarce-felt breezes pass.

Her tokens of renewing care
Hath Nature scattered everywhere,
In bud and flower, and warmer air.

But in their hour of bitterness,
What reck the broken Sokokis,
Beside their slaughtered chief, of this?

The turf's red stain is yet undried —
Scarce have the death-shot echoes died
Along Sebago's wooded side:

And silent now the hunters stand,
Grouped darkly, where a swell of land
Slopes upward from the lake's white sand.

Fire and the axe have swept it bare,
Save one lone beech, unclosing there
Its light leaves in the vernal air.

With grave, cold looks, all sternly mute,
They break the damp turf at its foot,
And bare its coiled and twisted root.

They heave the stubborn trunk aside,
The firm roots from the earth divide —
The rent beneath yawns dark and wide.

And there the fallen chief is laid,
In tasselled garb of skins arrayed,
And girded with his wampum-braid.

The silver cross he loved is pressed
Beneath the heavy arms, which rest
Upon his scarred and naked breast.[1]

---

[1] The Sokokis were early converts to the Catholic faith. Most of them, prior to the year 1756, had removed to the French settlements on the St. François.

'T is done: the roots are backward sent,
The beechen tree stands up unbent —
The Indian's fitting monument!

When of that sleeper's broken race
Their green and pleasant dwelling-place
Which knew them once, retains no trace;

O! long may sunset's light be shed
As now upon that beech's head —
A green memorial of the dead!

There shall his fitting requiem be,
In northern winds, that, cold and free,
Howl nightly in that funeral tree.

To their wild wail the waves which break
Forever round that lonely lake
A solemn under-tone shall make!

And who shall deem the spot unblest,
Where Nature's younger children rest,
Lulled on their sorrowing mother's breast?

Deem ye that mother loveth less
These bronzed forms of the wilderness
She foldeth in her long caress?

As sweet o'er them her wild flowers blow,
As if with fairer hair and brow
The blue-eyed Saxon slept below.

What though the places of their rest
No priestly knee hath ever pressed —
No funeral rite nor prayer hath blessed?

What though the bigot's ban be there,
And thoughts of wailing and despair,
And cursing in the place of prayer ![1]

Yet Heaven hath angels watching round
The Indian's lowliest forest-mound —
And *they* have made it holy ground.

There ceases man's frail judgment; all
His powerless bolts of cursing fall
Unheeded on that grassy pall.

O, peeled, and hunted, and reviled,
Sleep on, dark tenant of the wild!
Great Nature owns her simple child!

And Nature's God, to whom alone
The secret of the heart is known —
The hidden language traced thereon ;

Who from its many cumberings
Of form and creed, and outward things,
To light the naked spirit brings ;

[1] The brutal and unchristian spirit of the early settlers of New England toward the red man is strikingly illustrated in the conduct of the man who shot down the Sokokis chief. He used to say he always noticed the anniversary of that exploit, as " the day on which he sent the devil a present." — Williamson's *History of Maine.*

Not with our partial eye shall scan —
Not with our pride and scorn shall ban
The spirit of our brother man!

1841.

ST. JOHN.

[The fierce rivalship of the two French officers, left by the death of RAZILLA in the possession of Acadia, or Nova Scotia, forms one of the most romantic passages in the history of the New World. CHARLES ST. ESTIENNE, inheriting from his father the title of Lord DE LA TOUR, whose seat was at the mouth of the St. John's River, was a Protestant; DE AULNEY CHARNISY, whose fortress was at the mouth of the Penobscot, or ancient *Pentagoet*, was a Catholic. The incentives of a false religious feeling, sectarian intolerance, and personal interest and ambition, conspired to render their feud bloody and unsparing. The Catholic was urged on by the Jesuits, who had found protection from Puritan gallows-ropes under his jurisdiction ; the Huguenot still smarted under the recollection of his wrongs and persecutions in France. Both claimed to be champions of that cross from which went upward the holy petition of the Prince of Peace : "*Father, forgive them.*" LA TOUR received aid in several instances from the Puritan colonies of Massachusetts. During one of his voyages for the purpose of obtaining arms and provisions for his establishment at St. John, his castle was attacked by DE AULNEY, and successfully defended by its high-spirited mistress. A second attack, however, followed in the 4th mo. 1647. Lady LA TOUR defended her castle with a desperate perseverance. After a furious cannonade, DE AULNEY stormed the walls, and put the entire garrison to the sword. Lady LA TOUR languished a few days only in the hands of her inveterate enemy, and died of grief, greatly regretted by the colonists of Boston, to whom, as a devoted Protestant, she was well known.]

" To the winds give our banner !
    Bear homeward again ! "
Cried the lord of Acadia,
    Cried Charles of Estienne ;
From the prow of his shallop
    He gazed, as the sun,
From its bed in the ocean,
    Streamed up the St. John.

O'er the blue western waters
    That shallop had passed,
Where the mists of Penobscot
    Clung damp on her mast.
St. Saviour [1] had look'd
    On the heretic sail,
As the songs of the Huguenot
    Rose on the gale.

The pale, ghostly fathers
    Remembered her well,
And had cursed her while passing,
    With taper and bell,
But the men of Monhegan,[2]
    Of Papists abhorr'd,
Had welcomed and feasted
    The heretic Lord.

[1] The settlement of the Jesuits on the island of Mount Desert
was called St. Saviour.

[2] The isle of Monhegan was one of the first settled on the
coast of Maine.

They had loaded his shallop
    With dun-fish and ball,
With stores for his larder,
    And steel for his wall.
Pemequid, from her bastions
    And turrets of stone,
Had welcomed his coming
    With banner and gun.

And the prayers of the elders
    Had followed his way,
As homeward he glided,
    Down Pentecost Bay.
O! well sped La Tour!
    For, in peril and pain,
His lady kept watch
    For his coming again.

O'er the Isle of the Pheasant
    The morning sun shone,
On the plane trees which shaded
    The shores of St. John.
"Now, why from yon battlements
    Speaks not my love!
Why waves there no banner
    My fortress above?"

Dark and wild, from his deck
    St. Estienne gazed about,
On fire-wasted dwellings,
    And silent redoubt;

From the low, shattered walls
　　Which the flame had o'errun,
There floated no banner,
　　There thunder'd no gun!

But, beneath the low arch
　　Of its doorway there stood
A pale priest of Rome,
　　In his cloak and his hood.
With the bound of a lion,
　　La Tour sprang to land,
On the throat of the Papist
　　He fastened his hand.

"Speak, son of the Woman,
　　Of scarlet and sin!
What wolf has been prowling
　　My castle within?"
From the grasp of the soldier
　　The Jesuit broke,
Half in scorn, half in sorrow,
　　He smiled as he spoke:

"No wolf, Lord of Estienne,
　　Has ravaged thy hall,
But thy red-handed rival,
　　With fire, steel, and ball!
On an errand of mercy
　　I hitherward came,
While the walls of thy castle
　　Yet spouted with flame.

" Pentagoet's dark vessels
   Were moored in the bay,
Grim sea-lions, roaring
   Aloud for their prey."
" But what of my lady? "
   Cried Charles of Estienne :
" On the shot-crumbled turret
   Thy lady was seen :

" Half-veiled in the smoke-cloud,
   Her hand grasped thy pennon,
While her dark tresses swayed
   In the hot breath of cannon!
But woe to the heretic,
   Evermore woe!
When the son of the church
   And the cross is his foe!

" In the track of the shell,
   In the path of the ball,
Pentagoet swept over
   The breach of the wall!
Steel to steel, gun to gun,
   One moment — and then
Alone stood the victor,
   Alone with his men!

" Of its sturdy defenders,
   Thy lady alone
Saw the cross-blazon'd **banner**
   Float over St. John."

"Let the dastard look to it!"
　　Cried fiery Estienne,
"Were D'Aulney King Louis,
　　I'd free her again!"

"Alas, for thy lady!
　　No service from thee
Is needed by her
　　Whom the Lord hath set free:
Nine days, in stern silence,
　　Her thraldom she bore,
But the tenth morning came,
　　And Death opened her door!"

As if suddenly smitten
　　La Tour stagger'd back;
His hand grasped his sword-hilt,
　　His forehead grew black.
He sprang on the deck
　　Of his shallop again:
"We cruise now for vengeance!
　　Give way!" cried Estienne.

"Massachusetts shall hear
　　Of the Huguenot's wrong,
And from island and creek-side
　　Her fishers shall throng!
Pentagoet shall rue
　　What his Papists have done,
When his palisades echo
　　The Puritan's gun!"

O! the loveliest of heavens
Hung tenderly o'er him,
There were waves in the sunshine,
And green isles before him:
But a pale hand was beckoning
The Huguenot on;
And in blackness and ashes
Behind was St. John!

1841.

PENTUCKET.

[The village of Haverhill, on the Merrimack, called by the Indians Pentucket, was for nearly seventeen years a frontier town, and during thirty years endured all the horrors of savage warfare. In the year 1708, a combined body of French and Indians, under the command of De Challions, and Hertel de Rouville, the infamous and bloody sacker of Deerfield, made an attack upon the village, which at that time contained only thirty houses. Sixteen of the villagers were massacred, and a still larger number made prisoners. About thirty of the enemy also fell, and among them Hertel de Rouville. The minister of the place, Benjamin Rolfe, was killed by a shot through his own door.]

How sweetly on the wood-girt town
The mellow light of sunset shone!
Each small, bright lake, whose waters still
Mirror the forest and the hill,
Reflected from its waveless breast
The beauty of a cloudless West,
Glorious as if a glimpse were given
Within the western gates of Heaven,

Left, by the spirit of the star
Of sunset's holy hour, ajar!

Beside the river's tranquil flood
The dark and low-wall'd dwellings stood,
Where many a rood of open land
Stretch'd up and down on either hand,
With corn-leaves waving freshly green
The thick and blacken'd stumps between.
Behind, unbroken, deep and dread,
The wild, untravell'd forest spread,
Back to those mountains, white and cold,
Of which the Indian trapper told,
Upon whose summits never yet
Was mortal foot in safety set.

Quiet and calm, without a fear
Of danger darkly lurking near,
The weary laborer left his plough —
The milk-maid caroll'd by her cow —
From cottage door and household hearth
Rose songs of praise, or tones of mirth.
At length the murmur died away,
And silence on that village lay —
So slept Pompeii, tower and hall,
Ere the quick earthquake swallow'd all,
Undreaming of the fiery fate
Which made its dwellings desolate !

Hours pass'd away.   By moonlight sped
The Merrimack along his bed.
Bathed in the pallid lustre, stood
Dark cottage-wall and rock and wood,

Silent, beneath that tranquil beam,
As the hush'd grouping of a dream.
Yet on the still air crept a sound —
No bark of fox — nor rabbit's bound —
Nor stir of wings — nor waters flowing —
Nor leaves in midnight breezes blowing.

Was that the tread of many feet,
Which downward from the hillside beat?
What forms were those which darkly stood
Just on the margin of the wood? —
Charr'd tree-stumps in the moonlight dim,
Or paling rude, or leafless limb?
No — through the trees fierce eye-balls glow'd,
Dark human forms in sunshine show'd,
Wild from their native wilderness,
With painted limbs and battle-dress !

A yell, the dead might wake to hear,
Swell'd on the night air, far and clear —
Then smote the Indian tomahawk
On crashing door and shattering lock —
Then rang the rifle-shot — and then
The shrill death-scream of stricken men —
Sank the red axe in woman's brain,
And childhood's cry arose in vain —
Bursting through roof and window came,
Red, fast and fierce, the kindled flame ;
And blended fire and moonlight glared
On still dead men and weapons bared.

The morning sun looked brightly through
The river willows, wet with dew.

No sound of combat fill'd the air, —
No shout was heard, — nor gun-shot there:
Yet still the thick and sullen smoke
From smouldering ruins slowly broke,
And on the green sward many a stain,
And, here and there, the mangled slain
Told how that midnight bolt had sped,
Pentucket, on thy fated head !

Even now the villager can tell
Where Rolfe beside his hearth-stone fell,
Still show the door of wasting oak
Through which the fatal death-shot broke,
And point the curious stranger where
De Rouville's corse lay grim and bare —
Whose hideous head, in death still fear'd,
Bore not a trace of hair or beard —
And still, within the churchyard ground,
Heaves darkly up the ancient mound,
Whose grass-grown surface overlies
The victims of that sacrifice.

1838.

———◦◦◦———

THE FAMILIST'S HYMN.

[The " Pilgrims " of New England, even in their wilderness
home, were not exempted from the sectarian contentions
which agitated the mother country after the downfall of
Charles the First, and of the established Episcopacy. The
Quakers, Baptists, and Catholics were banished, on pain of
death, from the Massachusetts Colony. One Samuel Gorton,

a bold and eloquent declaimer, after preaching for a time in Boston, against the doctrines of the Puritans, and declaring that their churches were mere human devices, and their sacrament and baptism an abomination, was driven out of the State's jurisdiction, and compelled to seek a residence among the savages. He gathered round him a considerable number of converts, who, like the primitive Christians, shared all things in common. His opinions, however, were so troublesome to the leading clergy of the Colony, that they instigated an attack upon his "Family" by an armed force, which seized upon the principal men in it, and brought them into Massachusetts, where they were sentenced to be kept at hard labor in several towns (one only in each town), during the pleasure of the General Court, they being forbidden, under severe penalties, to utter any of their religious sentiments except to such ministers as might labor for their conversion. They were unquestionably sincere in their opinions, and, whatever may have been their errors, deserved to be ranked among those who have in all ages suffered for the freedom of conscience.]

FATHER ! to thy suffering poor
   Strength and grace and faith impart,
And with Thy own love restore
   Comfort to the broken heart!
Oh, the failing ones confirm
   With a holier strength of zeal! —
Give Thou not the feeble worm
   Helpless to the spoiler's heel!

Father ! for Thy holy sake
   We are spoiled and hunted thus ;
Joyful, for Thy truth we take
   Bonds and burthens unto us :

Poor, and weak, and robbed of all,
    Weary with our daily task,
That Thy truth may never fall
    Through our weakness, Lord, we ask

Round our fired and wasted homes
    Flits the forest-bird unscared,
And at noon the wild beast comes
    Where our frugal meal was shared;
For the song of praises there
    Shrieks the crow the livelong day,
For the sound of evening prayer
    Howls the evil beast of prey!

Sweet the songs we loved to sing
    Underneath Thy holy sky —
Words and tones that used to bring
    Tears of joy in every eye, —
Dear the wrestling hours of prayer,
    When we gathered knee to knee,
Blameless youth and hoary hair,
    Bow'd, O God, alone to Thee.

As Thine early children, Lord,
    Shared their wealth and daily bread,
Even so, with one accord,
    We, in love, each other fed.
Not with us the miser's hoard,
    Not with us his grasping hand;
Equal round a common board,
    Drew our meek and brother band!

Safe our quiet Eden lay
 When the war-whoop stirred the land,
And the Indian turn'd away
 From our home his bloody hand.
Well that forest-ranger saw,
 That the burthen and the curse
Of the white man's cruel law
 Rested also upon us.

Torn apart, and driven forth
 To our toiling hard and long,
Father! from the dust of earth
 Lift we still our grateful song!
Grateful — that in bonds we share
 In Thy love which maketh free;
Joyful — that the wrongs we bear,
 Draw us nearer, Lord, to Thee!

Grateful! — that where'er we toil —
 By Wachuset's wooded side,
On Nantucket's sea-worn isle,
 Or by wild Neponset's tide —
Still, in spirit, we are near,
 And our evening hymns which rise
Separate and discordant here,
 Meet and mingle in the skies!

Let the scoffer scorn and mock,
 Let the proud and evil priest
Rob the needy of his flock,
 For his wine-cup and his feast, —

Redden not Thy bolts in store
    Through the blackness of Thy skies?
For the sighing of the poor
    Wilt Thou not, at length, arise?

Worn and wasted, oh, how long
    Shall Thy trodden poor complain?
In Thy name they bear the wrong,
    In Thy cause the bonds of pain!
Melt oppression's heart of steel,
    Let the haughty priesthood see,
And their blinded followers feel,
    That in us they mock at Thee!

In Thy time, O Lord of hosts,
    Stretch abroad that hand to save
Which of old, on Egypt's coasts,
    Smote apart the Red Sea's wave!
Lead us from this evil land,
    From the spoiler set us free,
And once more our gather'd band,
    Heart to heart, shall worship Thee!

1838.

THE FOUNTAIN.

[On the declivity of a hill, in Salisbury, Essex County, is a beautiful fountain of clear water, gushing out from the very roots of a majestic and venerable oak. It is about two miles from the junction of the Powow River with the Merrimack.]

TRAVELLER! on thy journey toiling
    By the swift Powow,
With the summer sunshine falling
    On thy heated brow,

Listen, while all else is still
To the brooklet from the hill.

Wild and sweet the flowers are blowing
   By that streamlet's side,
And a greener verdure showing
   Where its waters glide —
Down the hill-slope murmuring on,
Over root and mossy stone.

Where yon oak his broad arms flingeth
   O'er the sloping hill,
Beautiful and freshly springeth
   That soft-flowing rill,
Through its dark roots wreath'd and bare,
Gushing up to sun and air.

Brighter waters sparkled never
   In that magic well,
Of whose gift of life for ever
   Ancient legends tell, —
In the lonely desert wasted,
And by mortal lip untasted.

Waters which the proud Castilian [1]
   Sought with longing eyes,
Underneath the bright pavilion
   Of the Indian skies;
Where his forest pathway lay
Through the blooms of Florida.

[1] De Soto, in the sixteenth century, penetrated into the wilds of the new world in search of gold and the fountain of perpetual youth.

Years ago a lonely stranger,
  With the dusky brow
Of the outcast forest-ranger,
  Crossed the swift Powow;
And betook him to the rill,
And the oak upon the hill.

O'er his face of moody sadness
  For an instant shone
Something like a gleam of gladness,
  As he stooped him down
To the fountain's grassy side
And his eager thirst supplied.

With the oak its shadow throwing
  O'er his mossy seat,
And the cool, sweet waters flowing
  Softly at his feet,
Closely by the fountain's rim
That lone Indian seated him.

Autumn's earliest frost had given
  To the woods below
Hues of beauty, such as Heaven
  Lendeth to its bow;
And the soft breeze from the west
Scarcely broke their dreamy rest.

Far behind was Ocean striving
  With his chains of sand;
Southward, sunny glimpses giving,
  'Twixt the swells of land,

Of its calm and silvery track,
Rolled the tranquil Merrimack.

Over village, wood and meadow,
    Gazed that stranger man
Sadly, till the twilight shadow
    Over all things ran,
Save where spire and westward pane
Flashed the sunset back again.

Gazing thus upon the dwelling
    Of his warrior sires,
Where no lingering trace was telling
    Of their wigwam fires,
Who the gloomy thoughts might know
Of that wandering child of woe?

Naked lay, in sunshine glowing,
    Hills that once had stood,
Down their sides the shadows throwing
    Of a mighty wood,
Where the deer his covert kept,
And the eagle's pinion swept !

Where the birch canoe had glided
    Down the swift Powow,
Dark and gloomy bridges strided
    Those clear waters now ;
And where once the beaver swam,
Jarred the wheel and frowned the dam.

For the wood-bird's merry singing,
    And the hunter's cheer,

Iron clang and hammer's ringing
    Smote upon his ear;
And the thick and sullen smoke
From the blackened forges broke.

Could it be, his fathers ever
    Loved to linger here?
These bare hills — this conquer'd river —
    Could they hold them dear,
With their native loveliness
Tamed and tortured into this?

Sadly, as the shades of even
    Gathered o'er the hill,
While the western half of Heaven
    Blushed with sunset still,
From the fountain's mossy seat
Turned the Indian's weary feet.

Year on year hath flown for ever,
    But he came no more
To the hill-side or the river
    Where he came before.
But the villager can tell
Of that strange man's visit well.

And the merry children, laden
    With their fruits or flowers —
Roving boy and laughing maiden,
    In their school-day hours,
Love the simple tale to tell
Of the Indian and his well.

1837.

THE EXILES.

[The incidents upon which the following ballad has its foundation, occurred about the year 1660. Thomas Macey was one of the first, if not *the* first white settler of Nantucket. A quaint description of his singular and perilous voyage, in his own hand-writing, is still preserved.]

THE goodman sat beside his door
  One sultry afternoon,
With his young wife singing at his side
  An old and goodly tune.

A glimmer of heat was in the air, —
  The dark green woods were still;
And the skirts of a heavy thunder-cloud
  Hung over the western hill.

Black, thick, and vast, arose that cloud
  Above the wilderness,
As some dark world from upper air
  Were stooping over this.

At times a solemn thunder pealed,
  And all was still again,
Save a low murmur in the air
  Of coming wind and rain.

Just as the first big rain-drop fell,
  A weary stranger came,
And stood before the farmer's door,
  With travel soiled and lame.

Sad seemed he, yet sustaining hope
   Was in his quiet glance,
And peace, like autumn's moonlight, clothed
   His tranquil countenance.

A look, like that his Master wore
   In Pilate's council-hall :
It told of wrongs — but of a love
   Meekly forgiving all.

"Friend! wilt thou give me shelter here?"
   The stranger meekly said ;
And, leaning on his oaken staff,
   The goodman's features read.

"My life is hunted — evil men
   Are following in my track ;
The traces of the torturer's whip
   Are on my aged back.

"And much, I fear, 'twill peril thee
   Within thy doors to take
A hunted seeker of the Truth,
   Oppressed for conscience' sake."

Oh, kindly spoke the goodman's wife —
   "Come in, old man!" quoth she, —
"We will not leave thee to the storm,
   Whoever thou may'st be."

Then came the aged wanderer in,
   And silent sat him down;
While all within grew dark as night
   Beneath the storm-cloud's frown.

But while the sudden lightning's blaze
   Filled every cottage nook,
And with the jarring thunder-roll
   The loosened casement shook,

A heavy tramp of horses' feet
   Came sounding up the lane,
And half a score of horse, or more,
   Came plunging through the rain.

" Now, Goodman Macey, ope thy door, —
   We would not be house-breakers;
A rueful deed thou'st done this day,
   In harboring banished Quakers."

Out looked the cautious goodman then,
   With much of fear and awe,
For there, with broad wig drenched with rain,
   The parish priest he saw.

" Open thy door, thou wicked man,
   And let thy pastor in,
And give God thanks, if forty stripes
   Repay thy deadly sin."

"What seek ye?" quoth the goodman,—
    "The stranger is my guest;
He is worn with toil and grievous wrong.—
    Pray let the old man rest."

"Now, out upon thee, canting knave!"
    And strong hands shook the door,
"Believe me, Macey," quoth the priest,—
    "Thou'lt rue thy conduct sore."

Then kindled Macey's eye of fire:
    "No priest who walks the earth,
Shall pluck away the stranger-guest
    Made welcome to my hearth."

Down from his cottage wall he caught
    The matchlock, hotly tried
At Preston-pans and Marston-moor,
    By fiery Ireton's side;

Where Puritan, and Cavalier,
    With shout and psalm contended;
And Rupert's oath, and Cromwell's prayer,
    With battle-thunder blended.

Up rose the ancient stranger then:
    "My spirit is not free
To bring the wrath and violence
    Of evil men on thee:

" And for thyself, I pray forbear, —
　　Bethink thee of thy Lord,
Who healed again the smitten ear,
　　And sheathed his follower's sword.

" I go, as to the slaughter led :
　　Friends of the poor, farewell ! "
Beneath his hand the oaken door
　　Back on its hinges fell.

" Come forth, old gray-beard, yea and nay ; "
　　The reckless scoffers cried,
As to a horseman's saddle-bow
　　The old man's arms were tied.

And of his bondage hard and long
　　In Boston's crowded jail,
Where suffering woman's prayer was heard,
　　With sickening childhood's wail,

It suits not with our tale to tell :
　　Those scenes have passed away —
Let the dim shadows of the past
　　Brood o'er that evil day.

" Ho, sheriff ! " quoth the ardent priest —
　　" Take goodman Macey too ;
The sin of this day's heresy,
　　His back or purse shall rue."

And priest and sheriff, both together
    Upon his threshold stood,
When Macey, through another door,
    Sprang out into the wood.

"Now, goodwife, haste thee!" Macey cried
    She caught his manly arm : —
Behind, the parson urged pursuit,
    With outcry and alarm.

Ho! speed the Maceys, neck or naught, —
    The river course was near : —
The plashing on its pebbled shore
    Was music to their ear.

A gray rock, tasselled o'er with birch,
    Above the waters hung,
And at its base, with every wave,
    A small light wherry swung.

A leap — they gain the boat — and there
    The goodman wields his oar :
"Ill luck betide them all " — he cried, —
    " The laggards upon the shore."

Down through the crashing under-wood,
    The burly sheriff came : —
"Stand, goodman Macey — yield thyself;
    Yield in the King's own name."

"Now out upon thy hangman's face!"
    Bold Macey answered then,—
"Whip *women*, on the village green,
    But meddle not with *men*."

The priest came panting to the shore,—
    His grave cocked hat was gone:
Behind him, like some owl's nest, hung
    His wig upon a thorn.

"Come back—come back!" the parson cried,
    "The church's curse beware."
"Curse an thou wilt," said Macey, "but
    Thy blessing prithee spare."

"Vile scoffer!" cried the baffled priest,—
    "Thou'lt yet the gallows see."
"Who's born to be hanged, will not be drowned,"
    Quoth Macey merrily;

"And so, sir sheriff and priest, good bye!"
    He bent him to his oar,
And the small boat glided quietly
    From the twain upon the shore.

Now in the west, the heavy clouds
    Scattered and fell asunder,
While feebler came the rush of rain,
    And fainter growled the thunder.

And through the broken clouds, the sun
　　Looked out serene and warm,
Painting its holy symbol-light
　　Upon the passing storm.

Oh, beautiful! that rainbow span,
　　O'er dim Crane-neck was bended; —
One bright foot touched the eastern hills,
　　And one with ocean blended.

By green Pentucket's southern slope
　　The small boat glided fast, —
The watchers of "the Block-house" saw
　　The strangers as they passed.

That night a stalwart garrison
　　Sat shaking in their shoes,
To hear the dip of Indian oars, —
　　The glide of birch canoes.

The fisher-wives of Salisbury,
　　(The men were all away),
Looked out to see the stranger oar
　　Upon their waters play.

Deer-Island's rocks and fir-trees threw
　　Their sunset-shadows o'er them,
And Newbury's spire and weathercock
　　Peered o'er the pines before them.

Around the Black Rocks, on their left,
    The marsh lay broad and green;
And on their right, with dwarf shrubs crowned,
    Plum Island's hills were seen.

With skilful hand and wary eye
    The harbor-bar was crossed;—
A plaything of the restless wave,
    The boat on ocean tossed.

The glory of the sunset heaven
    On land and water lay,—
On the steep hills of Agawam,
    On cape, and bluff, and bay.

They passed the gray rocks of Cape Ann,
    And Gloucester's harbor-bar;
The watch-fire of the garrison
    Shone like a setting star.

How brightly broke the morning
    On Massachusetts' Bay!
Blue wave, and bright green island,
    Rejoicing in the day.

On passed the bark in safety
    Round isle and headland steep—
No tempest broke above them,
    No fog-cloud veiled the deep.

Far round the bleak and stormy Cape
  The vent'rous Macey passed,
And on Nantucket's naked isle,
  Drew up his boat at last.

And how, in log-built cabin,
  They braved the rough sea-weather;
And there, in peace and quietness,
  Went down life's vale together:

How others drew around them,
  And how their fishing sped,
Until to every wind of heaven
  Nantucket's sails were spread:

How pale want alternated
  With plenty's golden smile;
Behold, is it not written
  In the annals of the isle?

And yet that isle remaineth
  A refuge of the free,
As when true-hearted Macey
  Beheld it from the sea.

Free as the winds that winnow
  Her shrubless hills of sand—
Free as the waves that batter
  Along her yielding land.

Than hers, at duty's summons,
No loftier spirit stirs, —
Nor falls o'er human suffering
A readier tear than hers.

God bless the sea-beat island! —
And grant for evermore,
That charity and freedom dwell,
As now upon her shore!

1841.

———◆◇◆———

THE NEW WIFE AND THE OLD.

[The following Ballad is founded upon one of the marvellous legends connected with the famous General M., of Hampton, N.H., who was regarded by his neighbors as a Yankee Faust, in league with the adversary. I give the story, as I heard it when a child, from a venerable family visitant.]

DARK the halls, and cold the feast —
Gone the bridesmaids, gone the priest!
All is over — all is done,
Twain of yesterday are one!
Blooming girl and manhood gray,
Autumn in the arms of May!

Hushed within and hushed without,
Dancing feet and wrestlers' shout;
Dies the bonfire on the hill;
All is dark and all is still,

Save the starlight, save the breeze
Moaning through the grave-yard trees;
And the great sea-waves below,
Like the night's pulse, beating slow.

From the brief dream of a bride
She hath wakened, at his side.
With half uttered shriek and start—
Feels she not his beating heart?
And the pressure of his arm,
And his breathing near and warm?

Lightly from the bridal bed
Springs that fair dishevelled head,
And a feeling, new, intense,
Half of shame, half innocence,
Maiden fear and wonder speaks
Through her lips and changing cheeks.

From the oaken mantel glowing
Faintest light the lamp is throwing
On the mirror's antique mould,
High-backed chair, and wainscot old,
And, through faded curtains stealing,
His dark sleeping face revealing.

Listless lies the strong man there,
Silver-streaked his careless hair;
Lips of love have left no trace
On that hard and haughty face;
And that forehead's knitted thought
Love's soft hand hath not unwrought.

"Yet," she sighs, "he loves me well,
More than these calm lips will tell
Stooping to my lowly state,
He hath made me rich and great,
And I bless him, though he be
Hard and stern to all save me!"

While she speaketh, falls the light
O'er her fingers small and white;
Gold and gem, and costly ring
Back the timid lustre fling —
Love's selectest gifts, and rare,
His proud hand had fastened there.

Gratefully she marks the glow
From those tapering lines of snow;
Fondly o'er the sleeper bending
His black hair with golden blending,
In her soft and light caress,
Cheek and lip together press.

Ha! — that start of horror! — Why
That wild stare and wilder cry,
Full of terror, full of pain?
Is there madness in her brain?
Hark! that gasping, hoarse and low:
"Spare me — spare me — let me go!"

God have mercy! — Icy cold
Spectral hands her own enfold,
Drawing silently from them
Love's fair gifts of gold and gem,

"Waken! save me!" still as death
At her side he slumbereth.

Ring and bracelet all are gone,
And that ice-cold hand withdrawn;
But she hears a murmur low,
Full of sweetness, full of woe,
Half a sigh and half a moan:
"Fear not! give the dead her own!"

Ah! — the dead wife's voice she knows!
That cold hand whose pressure froze,
Once in warmest life had borne
Gem and band her own hath worn.
"Wake thee! wake thee!"   Lo, his eyes
Open with a dull surprise.

In his arms the strong man folds her,
Closer to his breast he holds her;
Trembling limbs his own are meeting,
And he feels her heart's quick beating:
"Nay, my dearest, why this fear?"
"Hush!" she saith, "the dead is here!"

"Nay, a dream — an idle dream."
But before the lamp's pale gleam
Tremblingly her hand she raises, —
There no more the diamond blazes,
Clasp of pearl, or ring of gold, —
"Ah!" she sighs, "her hand was cold!"

Broken words of cheer he saith,
But his dark lip quivereth,
And as o'er the past he thinketh,
From his young wife's arms he shrinketh;
Can those soft arms round him lie,
Underneath his dead wife's eye?

She her fair young head can rest
Soothed and child-like on his breast,
And in trustful innocence
Draw new strength and courage thence;
He, the proud man, feels within
But the cowardice of sin!

She can murmur in her thought
Simple prayers her mother taught,
And His blessed angels call,
Whose great love is over all;
He, alone, in prayerless pride,
Meets the dark Past at her side!

One, who living shrank with dread,
From his look, or word, or tread,
Unto whom her early grave
Was as freedom to the slave,
Moves him at this midnight hour,
With the dead's unconscious power!

Ah, the dead, the unforgot!
From their solemn homes of thought,

Where the cypress shadows blend
Darkly over foe and friend,
Or in love or sad rebuke,
Back upon the living look.

And the tenderest ones and weakest,
Who their wrongs have borne the meekest,
Lifting from those dark, still places,
Sweet and sad-remembered faces,
O'er the guilty hearts behind
An unwitting triumph find.

1843.

VOICES OF FREEDOM.

------◆◇◆------

THE SLAVE SHIPS.

> " That fatal, that perfidious bark,
> Built i' the eclipse, and rigged with curses dark."
> *Milton's Lycidas.*

[The French ship Le RODEUR, with a crew of twenty-two men, and with one hundred and sixty negro slaves, sailed from Bonny, in Africa, April, 1819. On approaching the line, a terrible malady broke out — an obstinate disease of the eyes — contagious, and altogether beyond the resources of medicine. It was aggravated by the scarcity of water among the slaves (only half a wine-glass per day being allowed to an individual), and by the extreme impurity of the air in which they breathed. By the advice of the physician, they were brought upon deck occasionally ; but some of the poor wretches, locking themselves in each other's arms, leaped overboard, in the hope, which so universally prevails among them, of being swiftly transported to their own homes in Africa. To check this, the captain ordered several, who were stopped in the attempt, to be shot, or hanged, before their companions. The disease extended to the crew ; and one after another were smitten with it, until only *one* remained unaffected. Yet even this dreadful condition did not preclude calculation : to save the expense of supporting slaves rendered unsalable, and to obtain grounds for a claim against the underwriters, *thirty-six of the negroes, having become blind, were thrown into the sea and drowned !*

89

In the midst of their dreadful fears lest the solitary individual, whose sight remained unaffected, should also be seized
with the malady, a sail was discovered. It was the Spanish
slaver, LEON. The same disease had been there; and, horrible
to tell, all the crew had become blind! Unable to assist each
other, the vessels parted. The Spanish ship has never since
been heard of. The RODEUR reached Guadaloupe on the 21st
of June; the only man who had escaped the disease, and had
thus been enabled to steer the slaver into port, caught it in
three days after its arrival. — *Speech of M. Benjamin Constant,
in the French Chamber of Deputies,* June 17, 1820.]

"ALL ready?" cried the captain;
    "Ay, ay!" the seamen said;
"Heave up the worthless lubbers —
    The dying and the dead."
Up from the slave-ship's prison
    Fierce, bearded heads were thrust —
"Now let the sharks look to it —
    Toss up the dead ones first!"

Corpse after corpse came up, —
    Death had been busy there;
Where every blow is mercy,
    Why should the spoiler spare?
Corpse after corpse they cast
    Sullenly from the ship,
Yet bloody with the traces
    Of fetter-link and whip.

Gloomily stood the captain,
    With his arms upon his breast,
With his cold brow sternly knotted,
    And his iron lip compressed.

"Are all the dead dogs over?"
  Growled through that matted lip —
"The blind ones are no better,
  Let's lighten the good ship."

Hark! from the ship's dark bosom,
  The very sounds of hell!
The ringing clank of iron —
  The maniac's short, sharp yell! —
The hoarse, low curse, throat-stifled —
  The starving infant's moan —
The horror of a breaking heart
  Poured through a mother's groan!

Up from that loathsome prison
  The stricken blind ones came:
Below, had all been darkness —
  Above, was still the same.
Yet the holy breath of heaven
  Was sweetly breathing there,
And the heated brow of fever
  Cooled in the soft sea air.

"Overboard with them, shipmates!"
  Cutlass and dirk were plied;
Fettered and blind, one after one,
  Plunged down the vessel's side.
The sabre smote above —
  Beneath, the lean shark lay,
Waiting with wide and bloody jaw
  His quick and human prey.

God of the earth! what cries
    Rang upward unto Thee?
Voices of agony and blood,
    From ship-deck and from sea.
The last dull plunge was heard —
    The last wave caught its stain —
And the unsated shark looked up
    For human hearts in vain.

     *   *   *   *   *

Red glowed the western waters —
    The setting sun was there,
Scattering alike on wave and cloud
    His fiery mesh of hair.
Amidst a group in blindness,
    A solitary eye
Gazed, from the burdened slaver's deck,
    Into that burning sky.

" A storm," spoke out the gazer,
    " Is gathering and at hand —
Curse on't — I'd give my other eye
    For one firm rood of land."
And then he laughed — but only
    His echoed laugh replied —
For the blinded and the suffering
    Alone were at his side.

Night settled on the waters,
    And on a stormy heaven,
While fiercely on that lone ship's track
    The thunder-gust was driven.

"A sail! — thank God, a sail!"
    And, as the helmsman spoke,
Up through the stormy murmur,
    A shout of gladness broke.

Down came the stranger vessel
    Unheeding on her way,
So near, that on the slaver's deck
    Fell off her driven spray.
"Ho! for the love of mercy —
    We're perishing and blind!"
A wail of utter agony
    Came back upon the wind:

"Help *us!* for we are stricken
    With blindness every one;
Ten days we've floated fearfully,
    Unnoting star or sun.
Our ship's the slaver Leon —
    We've but a score on board —
Our slaves are all gone over —
    Help — for the love of God!"

On livid brows of agony
    The broad red lightning shone —
But the roar of wind and thunder
    Stifled the answering groan.
Wailed from the broken waters
    A last despairing cry,
As, kindling in the stormy light,
    The stranger ship went by.

☼   *   *   *   *

In the sunny Guadaloupe
  A dark-hulled vessel lay —
With a crew who noted never
  The night-fall or the day.
The blossom of the orange
  Was white by every stream,
And tropic leaf, and flower, and bird
  Were in the warm sun-beam.

And the sky was bright as ever,
  And the moonlight slept as well,
On the palm trees by the hill-side,
  And the streamlet of the dell;
And the glances of the Creole
  Were still as archly deep,
And her smiles as full as ever
  Of passion and of sleep.

But vain were bird and blossom,
  The green earth and the sky,
And the smile of human faces,
  To the slaver's darkened eye;
At the breaking of the morning,
  At the star-lit evening time,
O'er a world of light and beauty,
  Fell the blackness of his crime

1834.

STANZAS.

["The despotism which our fathers could not bear in their native country is expiring, and the sword of justice in her reformed hands has applied its exterminating edge to slavery. Shall the United States — the free United States, which could not bear the bonds of a king, cradle the bondage which a king is abolishing? Shall a Republic be less free than a Monarchy? Shall we, in the vigor and buoyancy of our manhood, be less energetic in righteousness than a kingdom in its age?" — *Dr. Follen's Address.*

"Genius of America! — Spirit of our free institutions — where art thou? — How art thou fallen, O Lucifer! son of the morning — how art thou fallen from Heaven! Hell from beneath is moved for thee, to meet thee at thy coming! — The kings of the earth cry out to thee, Aha! Aha! — ART THOU BECOME LIKE UNTO US?" — *Speech of Samuel J. May.*]

OUR fellow-countrymen in chains!
　　Slaves — in a land of light and law!
Slaves — crouching on the very plains
　　Where rolled the storm of Freedom's war!
A groan from Eutaw's haunted wood —
　　A wail where Camden's martyrs fell —
By every shrine of patriot blood,
　　From Moultrie's wall and Jasper's well!

By storied hill and hallowed grot,
　　By mossy wood and marshy glen,
Whence rang of old the rifle-shot,
　　And hurrying shout of Marion's men!

The groan of breaking hearts is there —
  The falling lash — the fetter's clank!
Slaves — SLAVES are breathing in that air,
  Which old De Kalb and Sumter drank!

What, ho! — *our* countrymen in chains!
  The whip on WOMAN's shrinking flesh!
Our soil yet reddening with the stains,
  Caught from her scourging, warm and fresh!
What! mothers from their children riven!
  What! God's own image bought and sold!
AMERICANS to market driven,
  And bartered as the brute for gold!

Speak! shall their agony of prayer
  Come thrilling to our hearts in vain?
To us whose fathers scorned to bear
  The paltry *menace* of a chain;
To us, whose boast is loud and long
  Of holy Liberty and Light —
Say, shall these writhing slaves of Wrong
  Plead vainly for their plundered Right?

What! shall we send, with lavish breath,
  Our sympathies across the wave,
Where Manhood, on the field of death,
  Strikes for his freedom, or a grave?
Shall prayers go up, and hymns be sung
  For Greece, the Moslem fetter spurning,
And millions hail with pen and tongue
  Our light on her altars burning?

Shall Belgium feel, and gallant France,
　　By Vendôme's pile and Schoenbrun's wall,
And Poland, gasping on her lance,
　　The impulse of our cheering call?
And shall the SLAVE, beneath our eye,
　　Clank o'er *our* fields his hateful chain?
And toss his fettered arms on high,
　　And groan for Freedom's gift, in vain?

Oh, say, shall Prussia's banner be
　　A refuge for the stricken slave?
And shall the Russian serf go free
　　By Baïkal's lake and Neva's wave?
And shall the wintry-bosomed Dane
　　Relax the iron hand of pride,
And bid his bondman cast the chain
　　From fettered soul and limb, aside?

Shall every flap of England's flag
　　Proclaim that all around are free,
From "farthest Ind" to each blue crag
　　That beetles o'er the Western Sea?
And shall we scoff at Europe's kings,
　　When Freedom's fire is dim with us,
And round our country's altar clings
　　The damning shade of Slavery's curse?

Go — let us ask of Constantine
　　To loose his grasp on Poland's throat;
And beg the lord of Mahmoud's line
　　To spare the struggling Suliote —

Will not the scorching answer come
    From turbaned Turk, and scornful Russ :
"Go, loose your fettered slaves at home,
    Then turn, and ask the like of us!"

Just God! and shall we calmly rest,
    The Christian's scorn — the heathen's mirth
Content to live the lingering jest
    And by-word of a mocking Earth?
Shall our own glorious land retain
    That curse which Europe scorns to bear?
Shall our own brethren drag the chain
    Which not even Russia's menials wear?

Up, then, in Freedom's manly part,
    From gray-beard eld to fiery youth,
And on the nation's naked heart
    Scatter the living coals of Truth!
Up — while ye slumber, deeper yet
    The shadow of our fame is growing!
Up — while ye pause, our sun may set
    In blood, around our altars flowing!

Oh! rouse ye, ere the storm comes forth —
    The gathered wrath of God and man —
Like that which wasted Egypt's earth,
    When hail and fire above it ran.
Hear ye no warnings in the air?
    Feel ye no earthquake underneath?
Up — up — why will ye slumber where
    The sleeper only wakes in death?

Up *now* for Freedom! — not in strife
   Like that your sterner fathers saw —
The awful waste of human life —
   The glory and the guilt of war:
But break the chain — the yoke remove,
   And smite to earth Oppression's rod,
With those mild arms of Truth and Love,
   Made mighty through the living God!

Down let the shrine of Moloch sink,
   And leave no traces where it stood;
Nor longer let its idol drink
   His daily cup of human blood:
But rear another altar there,
   To Truth and Love and Mercy given,
And Freedom's gift, and Freedom's prayer,
   Shall call an answer down from Heaven!

1834.

THE YANKEE GIRL.

SHE sings at her wheel, at that low cottage-door,
Which the long evening shadow is stretching before,
With a music as sweet as the music which seems
Breathed softly and faint in the ear of our dreams!

How brilliant and mirthful the light of her eye,
Like a star glancing out from the blue of the sky!
And lightly and freely her dark tresses play
O'er a brow and a bosom as lovely as they!

Who comes in his pride to that low cottage-door —
The haughty and rich to the humble and poor?
'T is the great Southern planter — the master who
  waves
His whip of dominion o'er hundreds of slaves.

"Nay, Ellen — for shame ! Let those Yankee fools
  spin,
Who would pass for our slaves with a change of
  their skin ;
Let them toil as they will at the loom or the wheel,
Too stupid for shame, and too vulgar to feel!

"But thou art too lovely and precious a gem
To be bound to their burdens and sullied by them —
For shame, Ellen, shame! — cast thy bondage aside,
And away to the South, as my blessing and pride.

" Oh, come where no winter thy footsteps can wrong,
But where flowers are blossoming all the year long,
Where the shade of the palm-tree is over my home,
And the lemon and orange are white in their bloom!

"Oh, come to my home, where my servants shall all
Depart at thy bidding and come at thy call ;
They shall heed thee as mistress with trembling and
  awe,
And each wish of thy heart shall be felt as a law."

Oh, could ye have seen her — that pride of our girls —
Arise and cast back the dark wealth of her curls,

With a scorn in her eye which the gazer could feel,
And a glance like the sunshine that flashes on steel!

"Go back, haughty Southron! thy treasures of gold
Are dim with the blood of the hearts thou hast sold;
Thy home may be lovely, but round it I hear
The crack of the whip and the footsteps of fear!

"And the sky of thy South may be brighter than
    ours,
And greener thy landscapes, and fairer thy flowers;
But, dearer the blast round our mountains which
    raves,
Than the sweet summer zephyr which breathes over
    slaves!

"Full low at thy bidding thy negroes may kneel,
With the iron of bondage on spirit and heel;
Yet know that the Yankee girl sooner would be
In fetters with them, than in freedom with thee!"

    1835.

———◆———

TO W. L. G.

CHAMPION of those who groan beneath
    Oppression's iron hand:
In view of penury, hate, and death,
    I see thee fearless stand,
Still bearing up thy lofty brow,
    In the steadfast strength of truth,
In manhood sealing well the vow
    And promise of thy youth.

Go on! — for thou hast chosen well;
  On in the strength of God!
Long as one human heart shall swell
  Beneath the tyrant's rod.
Speak in a slumbering nation's ear,
  As thou hast ever spoken,
Until the dead in sin shall hear —
  The fetter's link be broken!

I love thee with a brother's love,
  I feel my pulses thrill,
To mark thy spirit soar above
  The cloud of human ill.
My heart hath leaped to answer thine,
  And echo back thy words,
As leaps the warrior's at the shine
  And flash of kindred swords!

They tell me thou art rash and vain —
  A searcher after fame —
That thou art striving but to gain
  A long-enduring name —
That thou hast nerved the Afric's hand,
  And steeled the Afric's heart,
To shake aloft his vengeful brand,
  And rend his chain apart.

Have I not known thee well, and read
  Thy mighty purpose long!
And watched the trials which have made
  Thy human spirit strong?

And shall the slanderer's demon breath
　　Avail with one like me,
To dim the sunshine of my faith
　　And earnest trust in thee?

Go on — the dagger's point may glare
　　Amid thy pathway's gloom —
The fate which sternly threatens there
　　Is glorious martyrdom!
Then onward with a martyr's zeal —
　　Press on to thy reward —
The hour when man shall only kneel
　　Before his Father — God.

1833.

SONG OF THE FREE.

["Living, I shall assert the right of FREE DISCUSSION;
dying, I shall assert it; and, should I leave no other inheritance to my children, by the blessing of God I will leave them
the inheritance of FREE PRINCIPLES, and the example of a
manly and independent defence of them." — *Daniel Webster.*]

PRIDE of New England!
　　Soul of our fathers!
Shrink we all craven-like,
　　When the storm gathers?
What though the tempest be
　　Over us lowering,
Where's the New Englander
　　Shamefully cowering?

Graves green and holy
  Around us are lying,—
Free were the sleepers all,
  Living and dying!

Back with the Southerner's
  Padlocks and scourges!
Go — let him fetter down
  Ocean's free surges!
Go — let him silence
  Winds, clouds, and waters—
Never New England's own
  Free sons and daughters!
Free as our rivers are
  Oceanward going —
Free as the breezes are
  Over us blowing.

Up to our altars, then,
  Haste we, and summon
Courage and loveliness,
  Manhood and woman!
Deep let our pledges be:
  Freedom for ever!
Truce with oppression,
  Never, oh! never!
By our own birthright-gift,
  Granted of Heaven —
Freedom for heart and lip,
  Be the pledge given!

If we have whispered truth,
  Whisper no longer;

Speak as the tempest does,
   Sterner and stronger;
Still be the tones of truth
   Louder and firmer,
Startling the haughty South
   With the deep murmur:
God and our charter's right,
   Freedom for ever!
Truce with oppression,
   Never, oh! never!

1836.

THE HUNTERS OF MEN.

Written on reading the report of the proceedings of the American Colonization Society at its annual meeting in 1834.

HAVE ye heard of our hunting, o'er mountain and
   glen,
Through cane-brake and forest — the hunting of men?
The lords of our land to this hunting have gone,
As the fox-hunter follows the sound of the horn:
Hark! — the cheer and the hallo! — the crack of the
   whip,
And the yell of the hound as he fastens his grip!
All blithe are our hunters, and noble their match —
Though hundreds are caught, there are millions to
   catch.
So speed to their hunting, o'er mountain and glen,
Through cane-brake and forest — the hunting of
   men!

Gay luck to our hunters! — how nobly they ride
In the glow of their zeal, in the strength of their
      pride! —
The priest with his cassock flung back on the wind,
Just screening the politic statesman behind —
The saint and the sinner, with cursing and prayer —
The drunk and the sober, ride merrily there.
And woman — kind woman — wife, widow, and maid —
For the good of the hunted, is lending her aid:
Her foot's in the stirrup — her hand on the rein —
How blithely she rides to the hunting of men!

Oh! goodly and grand is our hunting to see,
In this "land of the brave and this home of the
      free."
Priest, warrior, and statesman, from Georgia to
      Maine,
All mounting the saddle — all grasping the rein —
Right merrily hunting the black man, whose sin
Is the curl of his hair and the hue of his skin!
Woe, now, to the hunted who turns him at bay!
Will our hunters be turned from their purpose and
      prey?
Will their hearts fail within them? — their nerves
      tremble, when
All roughly they ride to the hunting of men?

Ho! — ALMS for our hunters! all weary and faint
Wax the curse of the sinner and prayer of the saint.
The horn is wound faintly — the echoes are still,
Over cane-brake and river, and forest and hill.

Haste — alms for our hunters! the hunted once more
Have turned from their flight with their backs to the
    shore :
What right have *they* here in the home of the white,
Shadowed o'er by *our* banner of Freedom and
    Right?
Ho! — alms for the hunters! or never again
Will they ride in their pomp to the hunting of men!

ALMS — ALMS for our hunters! why *will* ye delay,
When their pride and their glory are melting away?
The parson has turned; for, on charge of his own,
Who goeth a warfare, or hunting, alone?
The politic statesman looks back with a sigh —
There is doubt in his heart — there is fear in his
    eye.
Oh! haste, lest that doubting and fear shall prevail,
And the head of his steed take the place of the tail.
Oh! haste, ere he leave us! for who will ride then,
For pleasure or gain, to the hunting of men?

    1835.

CLERICAL OPPRESSORS.

[In the Report of the celebrated pro-slavery meeting in
Charleston, S. C., on the 4th of the 9th month, 1835, published
in the "Courier" of that city, it is stated, "*The* CLERGY *of
all denominations attended in a body*, LENDING THEIR SANCTION
TO THE PROCEEDINGS, and adding by their presence to the
impressive character of the scene!"]

JUST God! — and these are they
Who minister at Thine altar, God of Right!
Men who their hands with prayer and blessing lay
    On Israel's Ark of light!

What! preach and kidnap men?
Give thanks — and rob Thy own afflicted poor?
Talk of Thy glorious liberty, and then
    Bolt hard the captive's door?

What! servants of Thy own
Merciful Son, who came to seek and save
The homeless and the outcast, — fettering down
    The tasked and plundered slave!

Pilate and Herod, friends!
Chief priests and rulers, as of old, combine!
Just God and holy! is that church, which lends
    Strength to the spoiler, Thine?

Paid hypocrites, who turn
Judgment aside, and rob the Holy Book
Of those high words of truth which search and burn
    In warning and rebuke;

Feed fat, ye locusts, feed!
And, in your tasselled pulpits, thank the Lord
That, from the toiling bondsman's utter need,
    Ye pile your own full board.

How long, O Lord! how long
Shall such a priesthood barter truth away,
And, in Thy name, for robbery and wrong
    At Thy own altars pray?

Is not Thy hand stretched forth
Visibly in the heavens, to awe and smite?
Shall not the living God of all the earth,
    And heaven above, do right?

Woe, then, to all who grind
Their brethren of a common Father down!
To all who plunder from the immortal mind
    Its bright and glorious crown!

Woe to the priesthood! woe
To those whose hire is with the price of blood —
Perverting, darkening, changing as they go,
    The searching truths of God!

Their glory and their might
Shall perish; and their very names shall be
Vile before all the people, in the light
    Of a world's liberty.

Oh! speed the moment on
When Wrong shall cease — and Liberty, and Love,
And Truth, and Right, throughout the earth be
    known
    As in their home above.

1836.

THE CHRISTIAN SLAVE.

[In a late publication of L. F. TASISTRO, " Random Shots and Southern Breezes," is a description of a slave auction at New Orleans, at which the auctioneer recommended the woman on the stand as " A GOOD CHRISTIAN ! "]

A CHRISTIAN! going, gone!
Who bids for God's own image? — for His grace
Which that poor victim of the market-place
    Hath in her suffering won?

    My God! can such things be?
Hast thou not said that whatsoe'er is done
Unto Thy weakest and Thy humblest one,
    Is even done to Thee?

    In that sad victim, then,
Child of Thy pitying love, I see Thee stand —
Once more the jest-word of a mocking band,
    Bound, sold, and scourged again!

    A Christian up for sale!
Wet with her blood your whips — o'ertask her
    frame,
Make her life loathsome with your wrong and
    shame,
    Her patience shall not fail!

A heathen hand might deal
Back on your heads the gathered wrong of years,
But her low, broken prayer and nightly tears
    Ye neither heed nor feel.

    Con well thy lesson o'er,
Thou *prudent* teacher -- tell the toiling slave
No dangerous tale of Him who came to save
    The outcast and the poor.

    But wisely shut the ray
Of God's free Gospel from her simple heart,
And to her darkened mind alone impart
    One stern command — "OBEY!" [1]

    So shalt thou deftly raise
The market price of human flesh : and while
On thee, their pampered guest, the planters smile,
    Thy church shall praise.

    Grave, reverend men shall tell
From Northern pulpits how thy work was blest,
While in that vile South Sodom, first and best,
    Thy poor disciples sell.

[1] There is in Liberty County, Georgia, an Association for the religious instruction of Negroes. Their seventh annual report contains an address by the *Rev.* Josiah Spry Law, from which we extract the following : — " There is a growing interest, in this community, in the religious instruction of Negroes. There is a conviction that religious instruction promotes the *quiet* and *order* of the people, and the pecuniary *interest* of the owners."

Oh, shame! the Moslem thrall,
Who, with his master, to the Prophet kneels,
While turning to the sacred Kebla feels
        His fetters break and fall.

Cheers for the turbaned Bey
Of robber-peopled Tunis! he hath torn
The dark slave-dungeons open, and hath borne
        Their inmates into day :

But our poor slave in vain
Turns to the Christian shrine his aching eyes —
Its rites will only swell his market price,
        And rivet on his chain.[1]

God of all right! how long
Shall priestly robbers at Thine altar stand,
Lifting in prayer to Thee, the bloody hand
        And haughty brow of wrong?

Oh, from the fields of cane,
From the low rice-swamp, from the trader's cell —
From the black slave-ship's foul and loathsome
        hell,
        And coffle's weary chain, —

---

[1] We often see advertisements in the Southern papers, in
which individual slaves, or several of a lot, are recommended
as "*pious*" or as "*members of churches.*" Lately we saw a
slave advertised, who, among other qualifications, was described as "*a Baptist preacher.*"

Hoarse, horrible, and strong,
Rises to Heaven that agonizing cry,
Filling the arches of the hollow sky,
    How LONG, OH GOD, HOW LONG?
1843.

STANZAS FOR THE TIMES.[1]

Is this the land our fathers loved,
    The freedom which they toiled to win?
Is this the soil whereon they moved?
    Are these the graves they slumber in?
Are *we* the sons by whom are borne
The mantles which the dead have worn?

And shall we crouch above these graves,
    With craven soul and fettered lip?
Yoke in with marked and branded slaves,
    And tremble at the driver's whip?
Bend to the earth our pliant knees,
And speak — but as our masters please?

[1] The "Times" alluded to were those evil times of the pro-slavery meeting in Faneuil Hall, for the suppression of freedom of speech, lest it should endanger the foundations of commercial society. In view of the outrages which a careful observation of the times had enabled him to foresee must spring from the false witness borne against the abolitionists by the speakers at that meeting well might Garrison say of them, "I consider the man who fires a city guiltless in comparison."

Shall outraged Nature cease to feel?
  Shall Mercy's tears no longer flow?
Shall ruffian threats of cord and steel —
  The dungeon's gloom — the assassin's blow,
Turn back the spirit roused to save
The Truth, our Country, and the Slave?

Of human skulls that shrine was made,
  Round which the priests of Mexico
Before their loathsome idol prayed —
  Is Freedom's altar fashioned so?
And must we yield to Freedom's God,
As offering meet, the negro's blood?

Shall tongues be mute, when deeds are wrought
  Which well might shame extremest hell?
Shall freemen lock the indignant thought?
  Shall Pity's bosom cease to swell?
Shall Honor bleed? — Shall Truth succumb?
Shall pen, and press, and soul be dumb?

No — by each spot of haunted ground,
  Where Freedom weeps her children's fall —
By Plymouth's rock, and Bunker's mound —
  By Griswold's stained and shattered wall —
By Warren's ghost — by Langdon's shade —
By all the memories of our dead!

By their enlarging souls, which burst
  The bands and fetters round them set —
By the free Pilgrim spirit nursed
  Within our inmost bosoms, yet, —
By all above — around — below —
Be ours the indignant answer — NO!

No — guided by our country's laws,
   For truth, and right, and suffering man,
Be ours to strive in Freedom's cause,
   As Christians *may* — as freemen *can*!
Still pouring on unwilling ears
That truth oppression only fears.

What! shall we guard our neighbor still,
   While woman shrieks beneath his rod,
And while he tramples down at will
   The image of a common God!
Shall watch and ward be round him set,
Of Northern nerve and bayonet?

And shall we know and share with him
   The danger and the growing shame?
And see our Freedom's light grow dim,
   Which should have filled the world with flame?
And, writhing, feel, where'er we turn,
A world's reproach around us burn?

Is 't not enough that this is borne?
   And asks our hearty neighbor more?
Must fetters which his slaves have worn,
   Clank round the Yankee farmer's door?
Must he be told beside his plough,
What he must speak, and when, and how?

Must he be told his freedom stands
   On Slavery's dark foundations strong —
On breaking hearts and fettered hands,
   On robbery, and crime, and wrong?
That all his fathers taught is vain —
That Freedom's emblem is the chain?

Its life — its soul, from slavery drawn?
    False — foul — profane!   Go — teach as well
Of holy Truth from Falsehood born!
    Of Heaven refreshed by airs from Hell!
Of Virtue in the arms of Vice!
Of Demons planting Paradise!

Rail on, then, " brethren of the South "—
    Ye shall not hear the truth the less —
No seal is on the Yankee's mouth,
    No fetter on the Yankee press!
From our Green Mountains to the Sea,
One voice shall thunder — WE ARE FREE!

    1835.

LINES.

Written on reading the spirited and manly remarks of Governor
   RITNER, of Pennsylvania, in his Message of 1836, on the
   subject of Slavery.

THANK God for the token! — one lip is still free —
One spirit untrammelled — unbending one knee!
Like the oak of the mountain, deep-rooted and firm,
Erect, when the multitude bends to the storm ;
When traitors to Freedom, and Honor, and God,
Are bowed at an Idol polluted with blood ;
When the recreant North has forgotten her trust,
And the lip of her honor is low in the dust, —
Thank God, that one arm from the shackle has
    broken!

Thank God, that one man, as a *freeman*, has spoken!
O'er thy crags, Alleghany, a blast has been blown!
Down thy tide, Susquehanna, the murmur has gone!
To the land of the South — of the charter and
    chain —
Of Liberty sweetened with Slavery's pain;
Where the cant of Democracy dwells on the lips
Of the forgers of fetters, and wielders of whips!
Where "chivalric" honor means really no more
Than scourging of women, and robbing the poor!
Where the Moloch of Slavery sitteth on high,
And the words which he utters are — WORSHIP, OR
    DIE!

Right onward, oh, speed it! Wherever the blood
Of the wronged and the guiltless is crying to God;
Wherever a slave in his fetters is pining;
Wherever the lash of the driver is twining;
Wherever from kindred, torn rudely apart,
Comes the sorrowful wail of the broken of heart;
Wherever the shackles of tyranny bind,
In silence and darkness, the God-given mind;
There, God speed it onward! — its truth will be
    felt —
The bonds shall be loosened — the iron shall melt!

And oh, will the land where the free soul of PENN
Still lingers and breathes over mountain and glen —
Will the land where a BENEZET'S spirit went forth
To the peeled, and the meted, and outcast of
    Earth —

Where the words of the Charter of Liberty first
From the soul of the sage and the patriot burst —
Where first for the wronged and the weak of their
    kind,
The Christian and statesman their efforts com-
    bined —
Will that land of the free and the good wear a
    chain?
Will the call to the rescue of Freedom be vain?

No, RITNER! — her "Friends," at thy warning shall
    stand
Erect for the truth, like their ancestral band;
Forgetting the feuds and the strife of past time,
Counting coldness injustice, and silence a crime;
Turning back from the cavil of creeds, to unite
Once again for the poor in defence of the Right;
Breasting calmly, but firmly, the full tide of Wrong,
Overwhelmed, but not borne on its surges along;
Unappalled by the danger, the shame, and the pain,
And counting each trial for Truth as their gain!

And that bold-hearted yeomanry, honest and true,
Who, haters of fraud, give to labor its due;
Whose fathers, of old, sang in concert with thine,
On the banks of Swetara, the songs of the Rhine —
The German-born pilgrims, who first dared to brave
The scorn of the proud in the cause of the slave: [1] —

---

[1] It is a remarkable fact that the first testimony of a religious
body against negro slavery was that of a Society of German
"Friends" in Pennsylvania.

Will the sons of such men yield the lords of the
    South
One brow for the brand — for the padlock one
    mouth?
They cater to tyrants? — they rivet the chain,
Which their fathers smote off, on the negro again?

No, never! one voice, like the sound in the cloud,
When the roar of the storm waxes loud and more loud,
Wherever the foot of the freeman hath pressed
From the Delaware's marge to the Lake of the West,
On the South-going breezes shall deepen and grow
Till the land it sweeps over shall tremble below!
The voice of a PEOPLE — uprisen — awake —
Pennsylvania's watchword, with Freedom at stake,
Thrilling up from each valley, flung down from each
    height,
"OUR COUNTRY AND LIBERTY! — GOD FOR THE
    RIGHT!"
  1837.

LINES.

Written on reading the famous " PASTORAL LETTER " of the
Massachusetts General Association, 1837.

So, this is all — the utmost reach
  Of priestly power the mind to fetter!
When laymen think — when women preach —
  A war of words — a "Pastoral Letter!"
Now, shame upon ye, parish Popes!
    Was it thus with those, your predecessors,
Who sealed with racks, and fire, and ropes
    Their loving kindness to transgressors?

A " Pastoral Letter," grave and dull —
    Alas! in hoof and horns and features,
How different is your Brookfield bull,
    From him who bellows from St. Peter's!
Your pastoral rights and powers from harm,
    Think ye, can words alone preserve them?
Your wiser fathers taught the arm
    And sword of temporal power to serve them.

Oh, glorious days — when church and state
    Were wedded by your spiritual fathers!
And on submissive shoulders sat
    Your Wilsons and your Cotton Mathers.
No vile " itinerant " then can mar
    The beauty of your tranquil Zion,
But at his peril of the scar
    Of hangman's whip and branding-iron.

Then, wholesome laws relieved the church
    Of heretic and mischief-maker,
And priest and bailiff joined in search,
    By turns, of Papist, witch, and Quaker!
The stocks were at each church's door,
    The gallows stood on Boston Common,
A Papist's ears the pillory bore, —
    The gallows-rope, a Quaker woman!

Your fathers dealt not as ye deal
    With " non-professing " frantic teachers;
They bored the tongue with red-hot steel,
    And flayed the backs of " female preachers."

Old Newbury, had her fields a tongue,
　And Salem's streets, could tell their story,
Of fainting woman dragged along,
　Gashed by the whip, accursed and gory!

And will ye ask me, why this taunt
　Of memories sacred from the scorner?
And why with reckless hand I plant
　A nettle on the graves ye honor?
Not to reproach New England's dead
　This record from the past I summon,
Of manhood to the scaffold led,
　And suffering and heroic woman.

No — for yourselves alone, I turn
　The pages of intolerance over,
That, in their spirit, dark and stern,
　Ye haply may your own discover!
For, if ye claim the "pastoral right"
　To silence Freedom's voice of warning,
And from your precincts shut the light
　Of Freedom's day around ye dawning;

If when an earthquake voice of power,
　And signs in earth and heaven are showing
That, forth, in its appointed hour,
　The Spirit of the Lord is going!
And, with that Spirit, Freedom's light
　On kindred, tongue, and people breaking,
Whose slumbering millions, at the sight,
　In glory and in strength are waking!

When for the sighing of the poor,
  And for the needy, God hath risen,
And chains are breaking, and a door
  Is opening for the souls in prison!
If then ye would, with puny hands,
  Arrest the very work of Heaven,
And bind anew the evil bands
  Which God's right arm of power hath riven —

What marvel that, in many a mind,
  Those darker deeds of bigot madness
Are closely with your own combined,
  Yet "less in anger than in sadness"?
What marvel, if the people learn
  To claim the right of free opinion?
What marvel, if at times they spurn
  The ancient yoke of your dominion?

Oh, how contrast, with such as ye,
  A LEAVITT's free and generous bearing!
A PERRY's calm integrity,
  A PHELP's zeal and Christian daring!
A FOLLEN's soul of sacrifice,
  And MAY's with kindness overflowing!
How green and lovely in the eyes
  Of freemen are their graces growing!

Ay, there's a glorious remnant yet,
  Whose lips are wet at Freedom's fountains,
The coming of whose welcome feet
  Is beautiful upon our mountains!

Men, who the gospel tidings bring
   Of Liberty and Love forever,
Whose joy is one abiding spring,
   Whose peace is as a gentle river!

But ye, who scorn the thrilling tale
   Of Carolina's high-souled daughters,
Which echoes here the mournful wail
   Of sorrow from Edisto's waters,
Close while ye may the public ear —
   With malice vex, with slander wound them —
The pure and good shall throng to hear,
   And tried and manly hearts surround them.

Oh, ever may the power which led
   Their way to such a fiery trial,
And strengthened womanhood to tread
   The wine-press of such self-denial,
Be round them in an evil land,
   With wisdom and with strength from Heaven,
With Miriam's voice, and Judith's hand,
   And Deborah's song for triumph given!

And what are ye who strive with God,
   Against the ark of his salvation,
Moved by the breath of prayer abroad,
   With blessings for a dying nation?
What, but the stubble and the hay
   To perish, even as flax consuming,
With all that bars His glorious way,
   Before the brightness of His coming?

And thou sad Angel, who so long
　　Hast waited for the glorious token,
That Earth from all her bonds of wrong
　　To liberty and light has broken —
Angel of Freedom! soon to thee
　　The sounding trumpet shall be given,
And over Earth's full jubilee
　　Shall deeper joy be felt in Heaven!

　1837.

LINES.

Written for the meeting of the Anti-Slavery Society, at Chatham Street Chapel, N.Y., held on the 4th of the 7th month, 1834.

O Thou, whose presence went before
　　Our fathers in their weary way,
As with Thy chosen moved of yore
　　The fire by night — the cloud by day!

When from each temple of the free,
　　A nation's song ascends to Heaven,
Most Holy Father! unto Thee
　　May not our humble prayer be given?

Thy children all — though hue and form
　　Are varied in Thine own good will —
With Thy own holy breathings warm,
　　And fashioned in Thine image still.

We thank Thee, Father!— hill and plain
  Around us wave their fruits once more,
And clustered vine, and blossomed grain,
  Are bending round each cottage door.

And peace is here; and hope and love
  Are round us as a mantle thrown,
And unto Thee, supreme above,
  The knee of prayer is bowed alone.

But oh, for those this day can bring,
  As unto us, no joyful thrill —
For those who, under Freedom's wing,
  Are bound in Slavery's fetters still:

For those to whom Thy living word
  Of light and love is never given —
For those whose ears have never heard
  The promise and the hope of Heaven!

For broken heart, and clouded mind,
  Whereon no human mercies fall —
Oh, be Thy gracious love inclined,
  Who, as a father, pitiest all!

And grant, O Father! that the time
  Of Earth's deliverance may be near,
When every land, and tongue, and clime,
  The message of Thy love shall hear —

When, smitten as with fire from heaven,
    The captive's chain shall sink in dust,
And to his fettered soul be given
    The glorious freedom of the just!

1834.

LINES.

Written for the celebration of the Third Anniversary of British
Emancipation, at the Broadway Tabernacle, N.Y., "First of
August," 1837.

O HOLY FATHER!—just and true
    Are all Thy works and words and ways,
And unto Thee alone are due
    Thanksgiving and eternal praise!
As children of Thy gracious care,
    We veil the eye — we bend the knee,
With broken words of praise and prayer,
    Father and God, we come to Thee.

For Thou hast heard, O God of Right,
    The sighing of the island slave;
And stretched for him the arm of might,
    Not shortened that it could not save.
The laborer sits beneath his vine,
    The shackled soul and hand are free —
Thanksgiving! — for the work is Thine!
    Praise! — for the blessing is of Thee!

And oh, we feel Thy presence here —
　　Thy awful arm in judgment bare!
Thine eye hath seen the bondman's tear —
　　Thine ear hath heard the bondman's prayer!
Praise! — for the pride of man is low,
　　The counsels of the wise are naught,
The fountains of repentance flow;
　　What hath our God in mercy wrought?

Speed on Thy work, Lord God of Hosts!
　　And when the bondman's chain is riven,
And swells from all our guilty coasts
　　The anthem of the free to Heaven,
Oh, not to those whom Thou hast led,
　　As with Thy cloud and fire before,
But unto Thee, in fear and dread,
　　Be praise and glory ever more.

1837.

------◆◇◆------

LINES.

**Written for the Anniversary celebration of the First of August,
at Milton, 1846.**

A FEW brief years have passed away
　　Since Britain drove her million slaves
Beneath the tropic's fiery ray:
God willed their freedom; and to-day
　　Life blooms above those island graves!

He spoke! across the Carib sea,
  We heard the clash of breaking chains,
And felt the heart-throb of the free,
The first, strong pulse of liberty
  Which thrilled along the bondman's veins.

Though long delayed, and far, and slow,
  The Briton's triumph shall be ours;
Wears slavery here a prouder brow
Than that which twelve short years ago
  Scowled darkly from her island bowers?

Mighty alike for good or ill
  With mother-land we fully share
The Saxon strength — the nerve of steel —
The tireless energy of will, —
  The power to do, the pride to dare.

What she has done can we not do?
  Our hour and men are both at hand;
The blast which Freedom's angel blew
O'er her green island, echoes through
  Each valley of our forest land.

Hear it, old Europe! we have sworn
  The death of slavery. —When it falls
Look to your vassals in their turn,
Your poor dumb millions, crushed and worn,
  Your prisons and your palace walls!

Oh kingly mockers! — scoffing show
   What deeds in Freedom's name we do ;
Yet know that every taunt ye throw
Across the waters, goads our slow
   Progression towards the right and true.

Not always shall your outraged poor,
   Appalled by democratic crime,
Grind as their fathers ground before, —
The hour which sees our prison door
   Swing wide shall be *their* triumph time.

Oh then, my brothers! every blow
   Ye deal is felt the wide earth through ;
Whatever here uplifts the low
Or humbles Freedom's hateful foe,
   Blesses the Old World through the New.

Take heart!   The promised hour draws near —
   I hear the downward beat of wings,
And Freedom's trumpet sounding clear —
Joy to the people! — woe and fear
   To new world tyrants, old world kings!

1846.

THE FAREWELL.

OF A VIRGINIA SLAVE MOTHER TO HER DAUGHTERS, SOLD
INTO SOUTHERN BONDAGE.

GONE, gone — sold and gone,
To the rice-swamp dank and lone.
Where the slave-whip ceaseless swings,
Where the noisome insect stings,
Where the fever demon strews
Poison with the falling dews,
Where the sickly sunbeams glare
Through the hot and misty air, —
Gone, gone — sold and gone,
To the rice-swamp dank and lone,
From Virginia's hills and waters, —
Woe is me, my stolen daughters!

Gone, gone — sold and gone,
To the rice-swamp dank and lone.
There no mother's eye is near them,
There no mother's ear can hear them ;
Never, when the torturing lash
Seams their back with many a gash,
Shall a mother's kindness bless them,
Or a mother's arms caress them.
Gone, gone — sold and gone,
To the rice-swamp dank and lone,
From Virginia's hills and waters —
Woe is me, my stolen daughters!

Gone, gone — sold and gone,
To the rice-swamp dank and lone.
Oh, when weary, sad, and slow,
From the fields at night they go,
Faint with toil, and racked with pain,
To their cheerless homes again —
There no brother's voice shall greet them —
There no father's welcome meet them.

Gone, gone — sold and gone,
To the rice-swamp dank and lone,
From Virginia's hills and waters —
Woe is me, my stolen daughters!

Gone, gone — sold and gone,
To the rice-swamp dank and lone,
From the tree whose shadow lay
On their childhood's place of play —
From the cool spring where they drank —
Rock, and hill, and rivulet bank —
From the solemn house of prayer,
And the holy counsels there —

Gone, gone — sold and gone,
To the rice-swamp dank and lone,
From Virginia's hills and waters, —
Woe is me, my stolen daughters!

Gone, gone — sold and gone,
To the rice-swamp dank and lone —
Toiling through the weary day,
And at night the spoiler's prey.
Oh, that they had earlier died,
Sleeping calmly, side by side,

Where the tyrant's power is o'er
And the fetter galls no more!
  Gone, gone — sold and gone,
  To the rice-swamp dank and lone,
  From Virginia's hills and waters, —
  Woe is me, my stolen daughters!

  Gone, gone — sold and gone,
  To the rice-swamp dank and lone.
By the holy love He beareth —
By the bruised reed He spareth —
Oh, may He, to whom alone
All their cruel wrongs are known,
Still their hope and refuge prove,
With a more than mother's love.
  Gone, gone — sold and gone,
  To the rice-swamp dank and lone,
  From Virginia's hills and waters, —
  Woe is me, my stolen daughters!

1838.

----◦◦----

ADDRESS.

Written for the opening of " PENNSYLVANIA HALL," dedicated
to Free Discussion, Virtue, Liberty, and Independence, on
the 15th of the 5th month, 1838.

NOT with the splendors of the days of old,
The spoil of nations, and "barbaric gold" —
No weapons wrested from the fields of blood,
Where dark and stern the unyielding Roman stood,
And the proud eagles of his cohorts saw
A world, war-wasted, crouching to his law —

Nor blazoned car — nor banners floating gay,
Like those which swept along the Appian way,
When, to the welcome of imperial Rome,
The victor warrior came in triumph home,
And trumpet-peal, and shoutings wild and high,
Stirred the blue quiet of the Italian sky;
But calm and grateful, prayerful and sincere,
As Christian freemen, only, gathering here,
We dedicate our fair and lofty Hall,
Pillar and arch, entablature and wall,
As Virtue's shrine — as Liberty's abode —
Sacred to Freedom, and to Freedom's God!

Oh! loftier halls, 'neath brighter skies than these,
Stood darkly mirrored in the Ægean seas,
Pillar and shrine — and life-like statues seen,
Graceful and pure, the marble shafts between,
Where glorious Athens from her rocky hill
Saw Art and Beauty subject to her will —
And the chaste temple, and the classic grove —
The hall of sages — and the bowers of love,
Arch, fane, and column, graced the shores, and gave
Their shadows to the blue Saronic wave;
And statelier rose, on Tiber's winding side,
The Pantheon's dome — the Coliseum's pride —
The Capitol, whose arches backward flung
The deep, clear cadence of the Roman tongue,
Whence stern decrees, like words of fate, went forth
To the awed nations of a conquered earth,
Where the proud Cæsars in their glory came,
And Brutus lightened from his lips of flame!

Yet in the porches of Athena's halls,
And in the shadows of her stately walls,
Lurked the sad bondman, and his tears of woe
Wet the cold marble with unheeded flow;
And fetters clanked beneath the silver dome
Of the proud Pantheon of imperious Rome.
Oh! not for him — the chained and stricken slave —
By Tiber's shore, or blue Ægina's wave,
In the thronged forum, or the sages' seat,
The bold lip pleaded, and the warm heart beat;
No soul of sorrow melted at his pain,
No tear of pity rusted on his chain!

But this fair Hall, to Truth and Freedom given,
Pledged to the Right before all Earth and Heaven,
A free arena for the strife of mind,
To caste, or sect, or color unconfined,
Shall thrill with echoes, such as ne'er of old
From Roman hall, or Grecian temple rolled;
Thoughts shall find utterance, such as never yet
The Propylæa or the Forum met.
Beneath its roof no gladiator's strife
Shall win applauses with the waste of life;
No lordly lictor urge the barbarous game —
No wanton Lais glory in her shame.
But here the tear of sympathy shall flow,
As the ear listens to the tale of woe;
Here, in stern judgment of the oppressor's wrong —
Shall strong rebukings thrill on Freedom's tongue —
No partial justice hold the unequal scale —
No pride of caste a brother's rights assail —
No tyrant's mandates echo from this wall,

Holy to Freedom and the Rights of All!
But a fair field, where mind may close with mind,
Free as the sunshine and the chainless wind;
Where the high trust is fixed on Truth alone,
And bonds and fetters from the soul are thrown;
Where wealth, and rank, and worldly pomp, and might,
Yield to the presence of the True and Right.

And fitting is it that this Hall should stand
Where Pennsylvania's Founder led his band,
From thy blue waters, Delaware! — to press
The virgin verdure of the wilderness.
Here, where all Europe with amazement saw
The soul's high freedom trammelled by no law;
Here, where the fierce and warlike forest-men
Gathered in peace, around the home of PENN,
Awed by the weapons Love alone had given,
Drawn from the holy armory of Heaven;
Where Nature's voice against the bondman's wrong
First found an earnest and indignant tongue;
Where LAY's bold message to the proud was borne,
And KEITH's rebuke, and FRANKLIN's manly scorn —
Fitting it is that here, where Freedom first
From her fair feet shook off the Old World's dust,
Spread her white pinions to our Western blast,
And her free tresses to our sunshine cast,
One Hall should rise redeemed from Slavery's ban —
One Temple sacred to the Rights of Man!

Oh! if the spirits of the parted come,
Visiting angels, to their olden home;
If the dead fathers of the land look forth

From their far dwellings, to the things of earth —
Is it a dream that with their eyes of love,
They gaze now on us from the bowers above?
LAY'S ardent soul — and BENEZET the mild,
Steadfast in faith, yet gentle as a child —
Meek-hearted WOOLMAN, — and that brother-band,
The sorrowing exiles from their "FATHERLAND,"
Leaving their homes in Krieshiem's bowers of vine,
And the blue beauty of their glorious Rhine,
To seek amidst our solemn depths of wood
Freedom from man and holy peace with God;
Who first of all their testimonial gave
Against the oppressor, — for the outcast slave, —
Is it a dream that such as these look down,
And with their blessing our rejoicings crown?

Let us rejoice, that, while the pulpit's door
Is barred against the pleaders for the poor;
While the church, wrangling upon points of faith,
Forgets her bondmen suffering unto death;
While crafty traffic and the lust of gain
Unite to forge oppression's triple chain,
One door is open, and one Temple free —
As a resting place for hunted Liberty!
Where men may speak, unshackled and unawed,
High words of truth, for Freedom and for God.

And when that truth its perfect work hath done,
And rich with blessings o'er our land hath gone;
When not a slave beneath his yoke shall pine,
From broad Potomac to the far Sabine;

When unto angel-lips at last is given
The silver trump of Jubilee to Heaven;
And from Virginia's plains — Kentucky's shades,
And through the dim Floridian everglades,
Rises, to meet that angel-trumpet's sound,
The voice of millions from their chains unbound —
Then, though this Hall be crumbling in decay,
Its strong walls blending with the common clay,
Yet, round the ruins of its strength shall stand
The best and noblest of a ransomed land —
Pilgrims, like those who throng around the shrine
Of Mecca, or of holy Palestine! —
A prouder glory shall that ruin own
Than that which lingers round the Parthenon.

Here shall the child of after years be taught
The work of Freedom which his fathers wrought —
Told of the trials of the present hour,
Our weary strife with prejudice and power, —
How the high errand quickened woman's soul,
And touched her lip as with a living coal —
How Freedom's martyrs kept their lofty faith,
True and unwavering, unto bonds and death. —
The pencil's art shall sketch the ruined Hall,
The Muses' garland crown its aged wall,
And History's pen for after times record
Its consecration unto FREEDOM'S GOD!

   1838.

THE MORAL WARFARE.

WHEN Freedom, on her natal day,
Within her war-rocked cradle lay,
An iron race around her stood,
Baptized her infant brow in blood
And, through the storm which round her swept,
Their constant ward and watching kept.

Then, where our quiet herds repose,
The roar of baleful battle rose,
And brethren of a common tongue
To mortal strife as tigers sprung,
And every gift on Freedom's shrine
Was man for beast, and blood for wine!

Our fathers to their graves have gone;
Their strife is past — their triumph won;
But sterner trials wait the race
Which rises in their honored place —
A moral warfare with the crime
And folly of an evil time.

So let it be.   In God's own might
We gird us for the coming fight,
And, strong in Him whose cause is ours
In conflict with unholy powers,
We grasp the weapons He has given, —
The Light, and Truth, and Love of Heaven!

    1836.

THE RESPONSE.

["To agitate the question (Slavery) anew, is not only impolitic, but it is a virtual breach of good faith to our brethren of the South; an unwarrantable interference with their domestic relations and institutions." "I can never, in the official station which I occupy, consent to *countenance* a course which may jeopard the peace and harmony of the Union." — *Governor Porter's Inaugural Message*, 1838.]

No "countenance" of his, forsooth!
    Who asked it at his vassal hands?
Who looked for homage done to Truth,
    By party's vile and hateful bands?
Who dreamed that one by them possessed,
Would lay for her his spear in rest?

His " countenance"! well, let it light
    The human robber to his spoil! —
Let those who track the bondman's flight,
    Like bloodhounds o'er our once free soil,
Bask in its sunshine while they may,
And howl its praises on their way;

We ask no boon: our rights we claim —
    Free press and thought — free tongue and pen —
The right to speak in Freedom's name,
    As Pennsylvanians and as men;
To do, by Lynch law unforbid,
What our own Rush and Franklin did.

Ay, there we stand, with planted feet,
  Steadfast, where those old worthies stood : —
Upon us let the tempest beat,
  Around us swell and surge the flood :
We fail or triumph on that spot ;
God helping us, we falter not.

"A breach of plighted faith?" For shame! —
  Who voted for that "breach"? Who gave
In the state councils, vote and name
  For freedom for the District slave?
Consistent patriot! go, forswear,
Blot out, "expunge" the record there![1]

Go, eat thy words. Shall H[enry] C[lay]
  Turn round — a moral harlequin?
And arch V[an] B[uren] wipe away
  The stains of his Missouri sin?
And shall that one unlucky vote
Stick, burr-like, in *thy* honest throat?

No — do thy part in "*putting down*"[2]
  The friends of Freedom : — summon out
The parson in his saintly gown,
  To curse the outlawed roundabout,
In concert with the Belial brood —
The Balaam of "the brotherhood"!

[1] It ought to be borne in mind that DAVID R. PORTER voted in the Legislature to instruct the congressional delegation of Pennsylvania to use their influence for the abolition of slavery in the District of Columbia.

[2] He [Martin Van Buren] thinks the abolitionists may be put down." — *Richmond (Va.) Enquirer.*

Quench every free discussion light —
   Clap on the legislative snuffers,
And caulk with " resolutions " tight
   The ghastly rents the Union suffers!
Let church and state brand Abolition
As heresy and rank sedition.

Choke down, at once, each breathing thing,
   That whispers of the Rights of Man : —
Gag the free girl who dares to sing
   Of freedom o'er her dairy pan : —
Dog the old farmer's steps about,
And hunt his cherished treason out.

Go, hunt sedition. — Search for that
   In every pedler's cart of rags ;
Pry into every Quaker's hat,
   And DOCTOR FUSSELL's saddle bags!
Lest treason wrap, with all its ills,
Around his powders and his pills.

Where Chester's oak and walnut shades
   With slavery-laden breezes stir,
And on the hills, and in the glades
   Of Bucks and honest Lancaster,
Are heads which think and hearts which feel —
Flints to the Abolition steel!

Ho! send ye down a corporal's guard
   With flow of flag and beat of drum —
Storm LINDLEY COATES's poultry yard,
   Beleaguer THOMAS WHITSON's home !
Beat up the Quaker quarters — show
Your valor to an unarmed foe!

Do more.   Fill up your loathsome jails
　　With faithful men and women — set
The scaffold up in these green vales,
　　And let their verdant turf be wet
With blood of unresisting men —
Ay, do all this, and more, — WHAT THEN?

Think ye, one heart of man and child
　　Will falter from his lofty faith,
At the mob's tumult, fierce and wild —
　　The prison cell — the shameful death?
No! — nursed in storm and trial long,
The weakest of our band is strong!

Oh! While before us visions come
　　Of slave ships on Virginia's coast —
Of mothers in their childless home,
　　Like Rachel, sorrowing o'er the lost —
The slave-gang scourged upon its way —
The bloodhound and his human prey —

We cannot falter!   Did we so,
　　The stones beneath would murmur out,
And all the winds that round us blow
　　Would whisper of our shame about.
No! let the tempest rock the land,
Our faith shall live — our truth shall stand.

True as the Vaudois hemmed around
　　With Papal fire and Roman steel —
Firm as the Christian heroine bound
　　Upon Domitian's torturing wheel,
We 'bate no breath — we curb no thought —
Come what may come, WE FALTER NOT!

THE WORLD'S CONVENTION.

OF THE FRIENDS OF EMANCIPATION, HELD IN LONDON IN 1840.

YES, let them gather! — Summon forth
The pledged philanthropy of Earth,
From every land, whose hills have heard
   The bugle blast of Freedom waking;
Or shrieking of her symbol bird
   From out his cloudy eyrie breaking;
Where Justice hath one worshipper,
Or Truth one altar built to her;
Where'er a human eye is weeping
   O'er wrongs which Earth's sad children know —
Where'er a single heart is keeping
   Its prayerful watch with human woe:
Thence let them come, and greet each other,
And know in each, a friend and brother!

Yes, let them come! from each green vale
   Where England's old baronial halls
   Still bear upon their storied walls
The grim crusader's rusted mail,
Battered by Paynim spear and brand
On Malta's rock or Syria's sand!
And mouldering pennon-staves once set
   Within the soil of Palestine,
By Jordan and Gennesaret;
   Or, borne with England's battle line,

O'er Acre's shattered turrets stooping,
Or, midst the camp their banners drooping,
   With dews from hallowed Hermon wet,
A holier summons now is given
   Than that gray hermit's voice of old,
Which unto all the winds of heaven
   The banners of the Cross unrolled!
Not for the long deserted shrine, —
   Not for the dull unconscious sod,
Which tells not by one lingering sigh
   That there the hope of Israel trod ; —
But for that TRUTH, for which alone
   In pilgrim eyes are sanctified
The garden moss, the mountain stone,
Whereon His holy sandals pressed —
The fountain which His lip hath blessed —
Whate'er hath touched his garment's hem
At Bethany or Bethlehem,
   Or Jordan's river side.
For FREEDOM, in the name of Him
   Who came to raise Earth's drooping poor,
To break the chain from every limb —
   The bolt from every prison door!
For these, o'er all the Earth hath passed
An ever-deepening trumpet blast,
As if an angel's breath had lent
Its vigor to the instrument.

And Wales, from Snowden's mountain wall,
Shall startle at that thrilling call,
   As if she heard her bards again ;
And Erin's " harp on Tara's wall "
   Give out its ancient strain,

Mirthful and sweet, yet sad withal —
    The melody which Erin loves,
When o'er that harp, mid bursts of gladness
And slogan cries and lyke-wake sadness,
    The hand of her O'Connell moves:
Scotland, from lake and tarn and rill,
And mountain hold, and heathery hill,
    Shall catch and echo back the note,
As if she heard upon her air
Once more her Cameronian's prayer
    And song of Freedom float.
And cheering echoes shall reply
From each remote dependency,
Where Britain's mighty sway is known,
In tropic sea or frozen zone;
Where'er her sunset flag is furling,
Or morning gun-fire's smoke is curling;
From Indian Bengal's groves of palm
And rosy fields and gales of balm,
Where Eastern pomp and power are rolled
Through regal Ava's gates of gold;
And from the lakes and ancient woods
And dim Canadian solitudes,
Whence, sternly from her rocky throne,
Queen of the North, Quebec looks down;
And from those bright and ransomed Isles
Where all unwonted Freedom smiles
And the dark laborer still retains
The scar of slavery's broken chains!

From the hoar Alps, which sentinel
The gateways of the land of Tell,
Where morning's keen and earliest glance

On Jura's rocky wall is thrown,
And from the olive bowers of France
   The vine groves garlanding the Rhone—
"Friends of the Blacks," as true and tried
As those who stood by Oge's side—
Brissot and eloquent Grégoire—
When with free lip and heart of fire
The Haytien told his country's wrong,
Shall gather at that summons strong—
Broglie, Passy, and him, whose song
Breathed over Syria's holy sod,
And in the paths which Jesus trod,
And murmured midst the hills which hem
Crownless and sad Jerusalem,
Hath echoes wheresoe'er the tone
Of Israel's prophet-lyre is known.

Still let them come — from Quito's walls,
   And from the Orinoco's tide,
From Lima's Inca-haunted halls,
From Santa Fe and Yucatan,—
   Men who by swart Guerrero's side
Proclaimed the deathless RIGHTS OF MAN,
   Broke every bond and fetter off,
   And hailed in every sable serf
A free and brother Mexican!
Chiefs who crossed the Andes' chain
   Have followed Freedom's flowing pennon,
And seen on Junin's fearful plain,
Glare o'er the broken ranks of Spain,
   The fire-burst of Bolivar's cannon!
And Hayti, from her mountain land,

Shall send the sons of those who hurled
Defiance from her blazing strand —
The war-gage from her Pétion's hand,
  Alone against a hostile world.

Nor all unmindful, thou, the while,
Land of the dark and mystic Nile! —
  Thy Moslem mercy yet may shame
  All tyrants of a Christian name —
When in the shade of Gezeh's pile,
Or, where from Abyssinian hills
El Gerek's upper fountain fills,
Or where from mountains of the Moon
El Abiad bears his watery boon,
Where'er thy lotos blossoms swim
  Within their ancient hallowed waters —
Where'er is heard thy prophet's hymn,
  Or song of Nubia's sable daughters,
The curse of SLAVERY and the crime,
Thy bequest from remotest time,
At thy dark Mehemet's decree
For evermore shall pass from thee ;
  And chains forsake each captive's limb
Of all those tribes, whose hills around
Have echoed back the cymbal sound
  And victor horn of Ibrahim.

And thou whose glory and whose crime
To earth's remotest bound and clime,
In mingled tones of awe and scorn,
The echoes of a world have borne,
My country ! glorious at thy birth,

A day-star flashing brightly forth, —
　The herald-sign of Freedom's dawn!
Oh! who could dream that saw thee then,
　And watched thy rising from afar,
That vapors from oppression's fen
　Would cloud the upward-tending star?
Or, that earth's tyrant powers, which heard,
　Awe-struck, the shout which hailed thy dawning,
Would rise so soon, prince, peer, and king,
To mock thee with their welcoming,
Like Hades when her thrones were stirred
　To greet the down-cast Star of Morning!
"Aha! and art thou fallen thus?
Art THOU become as one of *us?*"

Land of my fathers! — there will stand,
Amidst that world-assembled band,
Those owning thy maternal claim
Unweakened by thy crime and shame, —
The sad reprovers of thy wrong —
The children thou hast spurned so long.
Still with affection's fondest yearning
To their unnatural mother turning.
No traitors they! — but tried and leal,
Whose own is but thy general weal,
Still blending with the patriot's zeal
The Christian's love for human kind,
To caste and climate unconfined.

A holy gathering! — peaceful all —
No threat of war — no savage call
　For vengeance on an erring brother;

But in their stead the God-like plan
To teach the brotherhood of man
  To love and reverence one another,
As sharers of a common blood —
The children of a common God! —
Yet, even at its lightest word,
Shall Slavery's darkest depths be stirred :
Spain watching from her Moro's keep
Her slave-ships traversing the deep,
And Rio, in her strength and pride,
Lifting, along her mountain side,
Her snowy battlements and towers —
Her lemon groves and tropic bowers,
With bitter hate and sullen fear
Its freedom-giving voice shall hear ;
And where my country's flag is flowing,
On breezes from Mount Vernon blowing
  Above the Nation's council-halls,
Where Freedom's praise is loud and long,
  While, close beneath the outward walls,
The driver plies his reeking thong —
  The hammer of the man-thief falls,
O'er hypocritic cheek and brow
The crimson flush of shame shall glow :
And all who for their native land
Are pledging life and heart and hand —
Worn watchers o'er her changing weal,
Who for her tarnished honor feel —
Through cottage-door and council-hall
Shall thunder an awakening call.
The pen along its page shall burn
With all intolerable scorn —

And eloquent rebuke shall go
On all the winds that Southward blow;
From priestly lips now sealed and dumb,
Warning and dread appeal shall come,
Like those which Israel heard from him,
The Prophet of the Cherubim —
Or those which sad Esaias hurled
Against a sin-accursed world!
Its wizard-leaves the Press shall fling
Unceasing from its iron wing,
With characters inscribed thereon,
    As fearful in the despot's hall
As to the pomp of Babylon
    The fire-sign on the palace wall!
And, from her dark iniquities,
Methinks I see my country rise:
Not challenging the nations round
    To note her tardy justice done —
Her captives from their chains unbound,
    Her prisons opening to the sun; —
But tearfully her arms extending
Over the poor and unoffending;
    Her regal emblem now no longer
A bird of prey, with talons reeking,
Above the dying captive shrieking,
But, spreading out her ample wing —
A broad, impartial covering —
    The weaker sheltered by the stronger! —
Oh! then to Faith's anointed eyes
    The promised token shall be given;
And on a nation's sacrifice,
    Atoning for the sin of years,

And wet with penitential tears —
The fire shall fall from Heaven!
1839.

——•◦•——

NEW HAMPSHIRE. — 1845.

GOD bless New Hampshire! — from her granite
    peaks
Once more the voice of Stark and Langdon speaks.
The long-bound vassal of the exulting South
    For very shame her self-forged chain has bro-
    ken —
Torn the black seal of slavery from her mouth,
    And in the clear tones of her old time spoken!
Oh, all undreamed of, all unhoped-for changes! —
    The tyrant's ally proves his sternest foe;
To all his biddings, from her mountain ranges,
    New Hampshire thunders an indignant No!
Who is it now despairs? Oh, faint of heart,
    Look upward to those Northern mountains cold,
    Flouted by Freedom's victor-flag unrolled,
And gather strength to bear a manlier part!
All is not lost. The angel of God's blessing
    Encamps with Freedom on the field of fight;
Still to her banner, day by day, are pressing,
    Unlooked-for allies, striking for the right!
Courage, then, Northern hearts! — Be firm, be true:
What one brave State hath done, can ye not also
      do?

1845.

THE NEW YEAR:

ADDRESSED TO THE PATRONS OF THE PENNSYLVANIA
FREEMAN.

THE wave is breaking on the shore —
    The echo fading from the chime —
Again the shadow moveth o'er
    The dial-plate of time!

Oh, seer-seen Angel! waiting now
    With weary feet on sea and shore,
Impatient for the last dread vow
    That time shall be no more! —

Once more across thy sleepless eye
    The semblance of a smile has passed;
The year departing leaves more nigh
    Time's fearfullest and last.

Oh! in that dying year hath been
    The sum of all since time began —
The birth and death, the joy and pain,
    Of Nature and of Man.

Spring, with her change of sun and shower,
    And streams released from Winter's chain,
And bursting bud, and opening flower,
    And greenly-growing grain;

And Summer's shade, and sunshine warm,
  And rainbows o'er her hill-tops bowed,
And voices in her rising storm —
  God speaking from his cloud! —

And Autumn's fruits and clustering sheaves,
  And soft, warm days of golden light,
The glory of her forest leaves,
  And harvest-moon at night;

And Winter with her leafless grove,
  And prisoned stream, and drifting snow,
The brilliance of her heaven above
  And of her earth below: —

And man — in whom an angel's mind
  With earth's low instincts finds abode —
The highest of the links which bind
  Brute nature to her God;

His infant eye hath seen the light,
  His childhood's merriest laughter rung,
And active sports to manlier might
  The nerves of boyhood strung!

And quiet love, and passion's fires,
  Have soothed or burned in manhood's breast,
And lofty aims and low desires
  By turns disturbed his rest.

The wailing of the newly-born
  Has mingled with the funeral knell;

And o'er the dying's ear has gone
  The merry marriage-bell.

And Wealth has filled his halls with mirth,
  While Want, in many a humble shed,
Toiled, shivering by her cheerless hearth,
  The live-long night for bread.

And worse than all — the human slave —
  The sport of lust, and pride, and scorn!
Plucked off the crown his Maker gave —
  His regal manhood gone!

Oh! still my country! o'er thy plains,
  Blackened with slavery's blight and ban,
That human chattel drags his chains —
  An uncreated man!

And still, where'er to sun and breeze,
  My country, is thy flag unrolled,
With scorn, the gazing stranger sees
  A stain on every fold.

Oh, tear the gorgeous emblem down!
  It gathers scorn from every eye,
And despots smile, and good men frown,
  Whene'er it passes by.

Shame! shame! its starry splendors glow
  Above the slaver's loathsome jail —
Its folds are ruffling even now
  His crimson flag of sale.

Still round our country's proudest hall
  The trade in human flesh is driven,
And at each careless hammer-fall
  A human heart is riven.

And this, too, sanctioned by the men,
  Vested with power to shield the right,
And throw each vile and robber den
  Wide open to the light.

Yet shame upon them! — there they sit,
  Men of the North, subdued and still;
Meek, pliant poltroons, only fit
  To work a master's will.

Sold — bargained off for Southern votes —
  A passive herd of Northern mules,
Just braying through their purchased throats
  Whate'er their owner rules.

And he [1] — the basest of the base —
  The vilest of the vile — whose name,
Embalmed in infinite disgrace,
  Is deathless in its shame! —

A tool — to bolt the people's door
  Against the people clamoring there, —
An ass — to trample on their floor
  A people's right of prayer!

[1] The Northern author of the Congressional rule against
receiving petitions of the people on the subject of Slavery.

Nailed to his self-made gibbet fast,
    Self-pilloried to the public view —
A mark for every passing blast
    Of scorn to whistle through;

There let him hang, and hear the boast
    Of Southrons o'er their pliant tool —
A St. Stylites on his post,
    " Sacred to ridicule! "

Look we at home! — our noble hall,
    To Freedom's holy purpose given,
Now rears its black and ruined wall,
    Beneath the wintry heaven —

Telling the story of its doom —
    The fiendish mob — the prostrate law —
The fiery jet through midnight's gloom,
    Our gazing thousands saw.

Look to our State — the poor man's right
    Torn from him : — and the sons of those
Whose blood in Freedom's sternest fight
    Sprinkled the Jersey snows,

Outlawed within the land of Penn,
    That Slavery's guilty fears might cease,
And those whom God created men,
    Toil on as brutes in peace.

Yet o'er the blackness of the storm,
    A bow of promise bends on high,

And gleams of sunshine, soft and warm,
  Break through our clouded sky.

East, West, and North, the shout is heard,
  Of freemen rising for the right :
Each valley hath its rallying word —
  Each hill its signal light.

O'er Massachusetts' rocks of gray,
  The strengthening light of freedom shines,
Rhode Island's Narragansett Bay —
  And Vermont's snow-hung pines!

From Hudson's frowning palisades
  To Alleghany's laurelled crest,
O'er lakes and prairies, streams and glades,
  It shines upon the West.

Speed on the light to those who dwell
  In Slavery's land of woe and sin,
And through the blackness of that hell,
  Let Heaven's own light break in.

So shall the Southern conscience quake,
  Before that light poured full and strong,
So shall the Southern heart awake
  To all the bondman's wrong.

And from that rich and sunny land
  The song of grateful millions rise,
Like that of Israel's ransomed band
  Beneath Arabia's skies :

And all who now are bound beneath
　Our banner's shade — our eagle's wing,
From Slavery's night of moral death
　To light and life shall spring.

Broken the bondman's chain — and gone
　The master's guilt, and hate, and fear,
And unto both alike shall dawn,
　A New and Happy Year.

1839.

MASSACHUSETTS TO VIRGINIA.

[Written on reading an account of the proceedings of the citizens of Norfolk, Va., in reference to GEORGE LATIMER, the alleged fugitive slave, the result of whose case in Massachusetts will probably be similar to that of the negro SOMERSET in England, in 1772.]

THE blast from Freedom's Northern hills, upon its
　　Southern way,
Bears greeting to Virginia from Massachusetts
　　Bay : —
No word of haughty challenging, nor battle bugle's
　　peal,
Nor steady tread of marching files, nor clang of
　　horsemen's steel.

No trains of deep-mouthed cannon along our high-
　　ways go —
Around our silent arsenals untrodden lies the snow;

And to the land breeze of our ports, upon their
    errands far,
A thousand sails of commerce swell, but none are
    spread for war.

We hear thy threats, Virginia! thy stormy words
    and high,
Swell harshly on the Southern winds which melt
    along our sky;
Yet, not one brown, hard hand foregoes its honest
    labor here —
No hewer of our mountain oaks suspends his axe in
    fear.

Wild are the waves which lash the reefs along St.
    George's bank —
Cold on the shore of Labrador the fog lies white and
    dank;
Through storm, and wave, and blinding mist, stout
    are the hearts which man
The fishing-smacks of Marblehead, the sea-boats of
    Cape Ann.

The cold north light and wintry sun glare on their
    icy forms,
Bent grimly o'er their straining lines or wrestling
    with the storms;
Free as the winds they drive before, rough as the
    waves they roam,
They laugh to scorn the slaver's threat against their
    rocky home.

What means the Old Dominion? Hath she forgot
    the day
When o'er her conquered valleys swept the Briton's
    steel array?
How side by side, with sons of hers, the Massachu-
    setts men
Encountered Tarleton's charge of fire, and stout
    Cornwallis, then?

Forgets she how the Bay State, in answer to the
    call
Of her old House of Burgesses, spoke out from
    Faneuil Hall?
When, echoing back her Henry's cry, came pulsing
    on each breath
Of Northern winds, the thrilling sounds of "LIBERTY
    OR DEATH!"

What asks the Old Dominion? If now her sons
    have proved
False to their fathers' memory — false to the faith
    they loved;
If she can scoff at Freedom, and its great charter
    spurn,
Must we of Massachusetts from truth and duty
    turn?

We hunt your bondmen, flying from Slavery's hate-
    ful hell —
Our voices, at your bidding, take up the blood-
    hound's yell —

We gather, at your summons, above our fathers'
    graves,
From Freedom's holy altar-horns to tear your
    wretched slaves!

Thank God! not yet so vilely can Massachusetts
    bow;
The spirit of her early time is with her even now;
Dream not because her Pilgrim blood moves slow,
    and calm, and cool,
She thus can stoop her chainless neck, a sister's
    slave and tool!

All that a *sister* State should do, all that a *free* State
    may,
Heart, hand, and purse we proffer, as in our early
    day;
But that one dark loathsome burden ye must stagger
    with alone,
And reap the bitter harvest which ye yourselves
    have sown!

Hold, while ye may, your struggling slaves, and
    burden God's free air
With woman's shriek beneath the lash, and man-
    hood's wild despair;
Cling closer to the " cleaving curse " that writes upon
    your plains
The blasting of Almighty wrath against a land of
    chains.

Still shame your gallant ancestry, the cavaliers of
    old,
By watching round the shambles where human
    flesh is sold —
Gloat o'er the new-born child, and count his market
    value, when
The maddened mother's cry of woe shall pierce the
    slaver's den!

Lower than plummet soundeth, sink the Virginian
    name ;
Plant, if ye will, your fathers' graves with rankest
    weeds of shame ;
Be, if ye will, the scandal of God's fair universe —
We wash our hands forever, of your sin, and shame,
    and curse.

A voice from lips whereon the coal from Freedom's
    shrine had been,
Thrilled, as but yesterday, the hearts of Berkshire's
    mountain men :
The echoes of that solemn voice are sadly lingering
    still
In all our sunny valleys, on every wind-swept hill.

And when the prowling man-thief came hunting for
    his prey
Beneath the very shadow of Bunker's shaft of gray,
How, through the free lips of the son, the father's
    warning spoke ;
How, from its bonds of trade and sect, the Pilgrim
    city broke!

A hundred thousand right arms were lifted up on
    high, —
A hundred thousand voices sent back their loud
    reply ;
Through the thronged towns of Essex the startling
    summons rang,
And up from bench and loom and wheel her young
    mechanics sprang!

The voice of free, broad Middlesex — of thousands
    as of one —
The shaft of Bunker calling to that of Lexington —
From Norfolk's ancient villages ; from Plymouth's
    rocky bound
To where Nantucket feels the arms of ocean close
    her round ; —

From rich and rural Worcester, where through the
    calm repose
Of cultured vales and fringing woods the gentle
    Nashua flows,
To where Wachuset's wintry blasts the mountain
    larches stir,
Swelled up to Heaven the thrilling cry of " God save
    Latimer! "

And sandy Barnstable rose up, wet with the salt
    sea spray —
And Bristol sent her answering shout down Narra-
    gansett Bay!

Along the broad Connecticut old Hampden felt the
    thrill,
And the cheer of Hampshire's woodmen swept down
    from Holyoke Hill.

The voice of Massachusetts! Of her free sons and
    daughters —
Deep calling unto deep aloud — the sound of many
    waters!
Against the burden of that voice what tyrant power
    shall stand?
*No fetters in the Bay State! No slave upon her
    land!*

Look to it well, Virginians! In calmness we have
    borne,
In answer to our faith and trust, your insult and
    your scorn;
You've spurned our kindest counsels — you've hunted
    for our lives —
And shaken round our hearths and homes your
    manacles and gyves!

We wage no war — we lift no arm — we fling no
    torch within
The fire-damps of the quaking mine beneath your
    soil of sin;
We leave ye with your bondmen, to wrestle, while
    ye can,
With the strong upward tendencies and God-like
    soul of man!

But for us and for our children, the vow which we
    have given
For freedom and humanity, is registered in Heaven;
No slave-hunt in our borders — no pirate on our
    strand!
No fetters in the Bay State — no slave upon our land!

   1843.

———◆◆———

THE RELIC.

[PENNSYLVANIA HALL, dedicated to Free Discussion and
the cause of Human Liberty, was destroyed by a mob in 1838.
The following was written on receiving a cane wrought from
a fragment of the wood-work which the fire had spared.]

TOKEN of friendship true and tried,
   From one whose fiery heart of youth
With mine has beaten, side by side,
   For Liberty and Truth;
With honest pride the gift I take,
And prize it for the giver's sake.

But not alone because it tells
   Of generous hand and heart sincere;
Around that gift of friendship dwells
   A memory doubly dear —
Earth's noblest aim — man's holiest thought,
With that memorial frail inwrought!

Pure thoughts and sweet, like flowers unfold,
   And precious memories round it cling,

Even as the Prophet's rod of old
   In beauty blossoming :
And buds of feeling pure and good
Spring from its cold unconscious wood.

Relic of Freedom's shrine! — a brand
   Plucked from its burning! — let it be
Dear as a jewel from the hand
   Of a lost friend to me! —
Flower of a perished garland left,
Of life and beauty unbereft!

Oh! if the young enthusiast bears,
   O'er weary waste and sea, the stone
Which crumbled from the Forum's stairs,
   Or round the Parthenon ;
Or olive bough from some wild tree
Hung over old Thermopylæ :

If leaflets from some hero's tomb,
   Or moss-wreath torn from ruins hoary, —
Or faded flowers whose sisters bloom
   On fields renowned in story, —
Or fragment from the Alhambra's crest,
Or the gray rock by druids blessed ;

Sad Erin's shamrock greenly growing
   Where Freedom led her stalwart kern,
Or Scotia's " rough burr thistle " blowing
   On Bruce's Bannockburn —
Or Runnymede's wild English rose,
Or lichen plucked from Sempach's snows! —

If it be true that things like these
  To heart and eye bright visions bring,
Shall not far holier memories
  To this memorial cling?
Which needs no mellowing mist of time
To hide the crimson stains of crime!

Wreck of a temple, unprofaned —
  Of courts where Peace and Freedom trod,
Lifting on high, with hands unstained,
  Thanksgiving unto God;
Where Mercy's voice of love was pleading
For human hearts in bondage bleeding! —

Where midst the sound of rushing feet
  And curses on the night air flung,
That pleading voice rose calm and sweet
  From woman's earnest tongue;
And Riot turned his scowling glance,
Awed, from her tranquil countenance!

That temple now in ruin lies! —
  The fire-stain on its shattered wall,
And open to the changing skies
  Its black and roofless hall,
It stands before a nation's sight,
A grave-stone over buried Right!

But from that ruin, as of old,
  The fire-scorched stones themselves are crying,
And from their ashes white and cold
  Its timbers are replying!

A voice which slavery cannot kill
Speaks from the crumbling arches still!

And even this relic from thy shrine,
    Oh, holy Freedom! — hath to me
A potent power, a voice and sign
    To testify of thee;
And, grasping it, methinks I feel
A deeper faith, a stronger zeal.

And not unlike that mystic rod,
    Of old stretched o'er the Egyptian wave,
Which opened, in the strength of God,
    A pathway for the slave,
It yet may point the bondman's way,
And turn the spoiler from his prey.

1839.

------◆------

STANZAS FOR THE TIMES. — 1844.

[Written on reading the sentence of JOHN L. BROWN, of
South Carolina, to be executed on the 25th of 4th month, 1844,
for the crime of assisting a female slave to escape from bondage. The sentence was afterwards commuted.]

Ho! thou who seekest late and long
    A license from the Holy Book
For brutal lust and hell's red wrong,
    Man of the pulpit, look! —
Lift up those cold and atheist eyes,
    This ripe fruit of thy teaching see;

And teil us how to Heaven will rise
The incense of this sacrifice —
    This blossom of the Gallows Tree! —

Search out for SLAVERY'S hour of need
    Some fitting text of sacred writ;[1]
Give Heaven the credit of a deed
    Which shames the nether pit.
Kneel, smooth blasphemer, unto Him
    Whose truth is on thy lips a lie,
Ask that His bright-winged cherubim
May bend around that scaffold grim
    To guard and bless and sanctify! —

Ho! champion of the people's cause —
    Suspend thy loud and vain rebuke
Of foreign wrong and Old World laws,
    Man of the Senate, look! —
Was this the promise of the free, —
    The great hope of our early time, —
That Slavery's poison vine should be
Upborne by Freedom's prayer-nursed tree,
    O'erclustered with such fruits of crime? —

Send out the summons, East and West,
    And South and North, let all be there,
Where he who pitied the oppressed
    Swings out in sun and air.

[1] Three new publications, from the pens of Dr. Junkin,
President of Miami College, Alexander McCaine of the Meth-
odist Protestant church, and of a clergyman of the Cincinnati
Synod, defending Slavery on Scriptural ground, have recently
made their appearance.

Let not a democratic hand
    The grisly hangman's task refuse;
There let each loyal patriot stand
Awaiting Slavery's command
    To twist the rope and draw the noose!

But vain is irony — unmeet
    Its cold rebuke for deeds which start
In fiery and indignant beat
    The pulses of the heart.
Leave studied wit, and guarded phrase;
    And all that kindled heart can feel
Speak out in earnest words which raise,
Where'er they fall, an answering blaze,
    Like flints which strike the fire from steel.

Still let a mousing priesthood ply
    Their garbled text and gloss of sin,
And make the lettered scroll deny
    Its living soul within;
Still let the place-fed titled knave
    Plead Robbery's right with purchased lips,
And tell us that our fathers gave
For Freedom's pedestal, a slave,
    For frieze and moulding, chains and whips! —

But ye who own that higher law
    Whose tables in the heart are set,
Speak out in words of power and awe
    That God is living yet!
Breathe forth once more those tones sublime
    Which thrilled the burdened prophet's lyre,

And in a dark and evil time
Smote down on Israel's fast of crime
    And gift of blood, a rain of fire!

Oh, not for us the graceful lay,
    To whose soft measures lightly move
The Dryad and the woodland Fay,
    O'erlooked by Mirth and Love;
But such a stern and startling strain
    As Britain's hunted bards flung down
From Snowden, to the conquered plain,
Where harshly clanked the Saxon chain
    On trampled field and smoking town.

By Liberty's dishonored name,
    By man's lost hope, and failing trust,
By words and deeds, which bow with shame
    Our foreheads to the dust, —
By the exulting tyrant's sneer,
    Borne to us from the Old World's thrones,
And by their grief, who pining hear,
In sunless mines and dungeons drear,
    How Freedom's land her faith disowns; —

Speak out in *acts*; the time for words
    Has passed, and deeds alone suffice;
In the loud clang of meeting swords
    The softer music dies!
Act — act, in God's name, while ye may,
    Smite from the church her leprous limb,
Throw open to the light of day

The bondman's cell, and break away
    The chains the state has bound on him.

Ho! every true and living soul,
    To Freedom's perilled altar bear
The freeman's and the Christian's whole,
    Tongue, pen, and vote, and prayer!
One last great battle for the Right, —
    One short, sharp struggle to be free!
To do is to succeed — our fight
Is waged in Heaven's approving sight —
    The smile of God is Victory!

1844.

THE BRANDED HAND.

[CAPTAIN JONATHAN WALKER, of Harwich, Mass., was solicited by several fugitive slaves at Pensacola, Florida, to convey them in his vessel to the British West Indies. Although well aware of the hazard of the enterprise, he attempted to comply with their request. He was seized by an American vessel, consigned to the American authorities at Key West, and by them taken back to Florida — where, after a long and rigorous imprisonment he was brought to trial. He was sentenced to be branded on the right hand with the letters "S. S." ("Slave Stealer") and amerced in a heavy fine. He was released on the payment of his fine in the 6th month of 1845.]

WELCOME home again, brave seaman! with thy
        thoughtful brow and gray,
And the old heroic spirit of our earlier, better day —

With that front of calm endurance, on whose steady
    nerve, in vain
Pressed the iron of the prison, smote the fiery shafts
    of pain!

Is the tyrant's brand upon thee? Did the brutal
    cravens aim
To make God's truth thy falsehood, His holiest work
    thy shame?
When, all blood-quenched, from the torture the iron
    was withdrawn,
How laughed their evil angel the baffled fools to
    scorn!

They change to wrong, the duty which God hath
    written out
On the great heart of humanity too legible for
    doubt!
They, the loathsome moral lepers, blotched from
    footsole up to crown,
Give to shame what God hath given unto honor and
    renown!

Why, that brand is highest honor! — than its traces
    never yet
Upon old armorial hatchments was a prouder blazon
    set ;
And thy unborn generations, as they tread our rocky
    strand,
Shall tell with pride the story of their father's
    BRANDED HAND!

As the Templar home was welcomed, bearing back
  from Syrian wars
The scars of Arab lances, and of Paynim scimitars.
The pallor of the prison and the shackle's crimson
  span,
So we meet thee, so we greet thee, truest friend of
  God and man!

He suffered for the ransom of the dear Redeemer's
  grave,
Thou for His living presence in the bound and
  bleeding slave;
He for a soil no longer by the feet of angels trod,
Thou for the true Shechinah, the present home of God!

For, while the jurist sitting with the slave-whip o'er
  him swung,
From the tortured truths of freedom the lie of slavery
  wrung,
And the solemn priest to Moloch, on each God-
  deserted shrine,
Broke the bondman's heart for bread, poured the
  bondman's blood for wine —

While the multitude in blindness to a far-off Saviour
  knelt,
And spurned, the while, the temple where a present
  Saviour dwelt;
Thou beheld'st Him in the task-field, in the prison
  shadows dim,
And thy mercy to the bondman, it was mercy unto
  Him!

In the lone and long night watches, sky above and
    wave below,
Thou did'st learn a higher wisdom than the babbling
    school-men know ;
God's stars and silence taught thee, as His angels
    only can,
That the one, sole sacred thing beneath the cope of
    heaven is Man!

That he who treads profanely on the scrolls of law
    and creed,
In the depth of God's great goodness may find mercy
    in his need ;
But woe to him who crushes the SOUL with chain
    and rod,
And herds with lower natures the awful form of
    God!

Then lift thy manly right hand, bold ploughman of
    the wave!
Its branded palm shall prophesy, "SALVATION TO
    THE SLAVE!"
Hold up its fire-wrought language, that whoso reads
    may feel
His heart swell strong within him, his sinews change
    to steel.

Hold it up before our sunshine, up against our North-
    ern air —
Ho! men of Massachusetts, for the love of God look
    there!

Take it henceforth for your standard — like the
 Bruce's heart of yore,
In the dark strife closing round ye, let that hand be
 seen before!

And the tyrants of the slave-land shall tremble at
 that sign,
When it points its finger Southward along the Puritan line :
Woe to the State-gorged leeches, and the Church's
 locust band,
When they look from slavery's ramparts on the coming of that hand!

 1846.

TEXAS.

VOICE OF NEW ENGLAND.

Up the hill-side, down the glen,
Rouse the sleeping citizen ;
Summon out the might of men!

Like a lion growling low —
Like a night-storm rising slow —
Like the tread of unseen foe —

It is coming — it is nigh!
Stand your homes and altars by ;
On your own free thresholds die!

Clang the bells in all your spires;
On the gray hills of your sires
Fling to heaven your signal fires!

From Wachuset, lone and bleak,
Unto Berkshire's tallest peak,
Let the flame-tongued heralds speak!

O! for God and duty stand,
Heart to heart and hand to hand,
Round the old graves of the land!

Whoso shrinks or falters now,
Whoso to the yoke would bow,
Brand the craven on his brow!

Freedom's soil hath only place
For a free and fearless race —
None for traitors false and base.

Perish party — perish clan;
Strike together while ye can,
Like the arm of one strong man!

Like that angel's voice sublime,
Heard above a world of crime.
Crying of the end of time —

With one heart and with one mouth,
Let the North unto the South
Speak the word befitting both:

" What though Issachar be strong!
    Ye may load his back with wrong
    Overmuch and over long:

" Patience with her cup o'errun,
    With her weary thread outspun,
    Murmurs that her work is done.

" Make our Union-bond a chain,
    Weak as tow in Freedom's strain
    Link by link shall snap in twain.

" Vainly shall your sand-wrought rope
    Bind the starry cluster up,
    Shattered over heaven's blue cope!

" Give us bright though broken rays,
    Rather than eternal haze,
    Clouding o'er the full-orbed blaze!

" Take your land of sun and bloom;
    Only leave to Freedom room
    For her plough, and forge, and loom;

" Take your slavery-blackened vales;
    Leave us but our own free gales,
    Blowing on our thousand sails!

" Boldly, or with treacherous art,
    Strike the blood-wrought chain apart;
    Break the Union's mighty heart;

"Work the ruin, if ye will;
  Pluck upon your heads an ill
  Which shall grow and deepen still!

" With your bondman's right arm bare,
  With his heart of black despair,
  Stand alone, if stand ye dare!

" Onward with your fell design;
  Dig the gulf and draw the line:
  Fire beneath your feet the mine:

" Deeply, when the wide abyss
  Yawns between your land and this,
  Shall ye feel your helplessness.

" By the hearth, and in the bed,
  Shaken by a look or tread,
  Ye shall own a guilty dread.

" And the curse of unpaid toil,
  Downward through your generous soil
  Like a fire shall burn and spoil.

" Our bleak hills shall bud and blow,
  Vines our rocks shall overgrow,
  Plenty in our valleys flow; —

" And when vengeance clouds your skies,
  Hither shall ye turn your eyes,
  As the lost on Paradise!

"We but ask our rocky strand,
　　Freedom's true and brother band,
　　Freedom's strong and honest hand, —

"Valleys by the slave untrod,
　　And the Pilgrim's mountain sod,
　　Blessed of our fathers' God!"

1844.

TO FANEUIL HALL.

[Written in 1844, on reading a call by "a Massachusetts Freeman" for a meeting in Faneuil Hall of the citizens of Massachusetts, without distinction of party, opposed to the annexation of Texas, and the aggressions of South Carolina, and in favor of decisive action against Slavery.]

MEN! — if manhood still ye claim,
　　If the Northern pulse can thrill,
Roused by wrong or stung by shame,
　　Freely, strongly still : —
Let the sounds of traffic die :
　　Shut the mill-gate — leave the stall —
Fling the axe and hammer by —
　　Throng to Faneuil Hall!

Wrongs which freemen never brooked —
　　Dangers grim and fierce as they,
Which, like couching lions, looked
　　On your fathers' way ; —

These your instant zeal demand,
  Shaking with their earthquake-call
Every rood of Pilgrim land —
  Ho, to Faneuil Hall!

From your capes and sandy bars —
  From your mountain-ridges cold,
Through whose pines the westering stars
  Stoop their crowns of gold —
Come, and with your footsteps wake
  Echoes from that holy wall:
Once again, for Freedom's sake,
  Rock your fathers' hall!

Up, and tread beneath your feet
  Every cord by party spun;
Let your hearts together beat
  As the heart of one.
Banks and tariffs, stocks and trade,
  Let them rise or let them fall:
Freedom asks your common aid —
  Up, to Faneuil Hall!

Up, and let each voice that speaks
  Ring from thence to Southern plains,
Sharply as the blow which breaks
  Prison-bolts and chains!
Speak as well becomes the free —
  Dreaded more than steel or ball,
Shall your calmest utterance be,
  Heard from Faneuil Hall!

Have they wronged us?   Let us then
    Render back nor threats nor prayers;
Have they chained our free-born men?
    LET US UNCHAIN THEIRS!
Up! your banner leads the van,
    Blazoned "Liberty for all!"
Finish what your sires began —
    Up, to Faneuil Hall!

1844.

TO MASSACHUSETTS.

WRITTEN DURING THE PENDING OF THE TEXAS
QUESTION.

WHAT though around thee blazes
    No fiery rallying sign?
From all thy own high places,
    Give heaven the light of thine!
What though unthrilled, unmoving,
    The statesman stands apart,
And comes no warm approving
    From Mammon's crowded mart?

Still let the land be shaken
    By a summons of thine own!
By all save truth forsaken,
    Why, stand with that alone!
Shrink not from strife unequal!
    With the best is always hope;
And ever in the sequel
    God holds the right side up!

But when, with thine uniting,
  Come voices long and loud,
And far-off hills are writing
  Thy fire-words on the cloud:
When from Penobscot's fountains
  A deep response is heard,
And across the Western mountains
  Rolls back thy rallying word;

Shall thy line of battle falter,
  With its allies just in view?
Oh, by hearth and holy altar,
  My Fatherland, be true!
Fling abroad thy scrolls of Freedom!
  Speed them onward far and fast!
Over hill and valley speed them,
  Like the Sibyl's on the blast!

Lo! the Empire State is shaking
  The shackles from her hand;
With the rugged North is waking
  The level sunset land!
On they come — the free battalions!
  East and West and North they
And the heart-beat of the millions
  Is the beat of Freedom's drum.

"To the tyrant's plot no favor!
  No heed to place-fed knaves!
Bar and bolt the door forever
  Against the land of Slaves!"

Hear it, mother Earth, and hear it.
　　The Heavens above us spread!
The land is roused — its spirit
　　Was sleeping, but not dead!

1844.

　　　　　—◦∗◦—

THE PINE TREE.

Written on hearing that the Anti-Slavery Resolves of STEPHEN C. PHILLIPS had been rejected by the Whig Convention in Faneuil Hall, in 1846.

LIFT again the stately emblem on the Bay State's
　　rusted shield,
Give to Northern winds the Pine Tree on our ban-
　　ner's tattered field,
Sons of men who sat in council with their Bibles
　　round the board,
Answering England's royal missive with a firm,
　　"THUS SAITH THE LORD!"
Rise again for home and freedom! — set the battle
　　in array! —
What the fathers did of old time we their sons
　　must do to-day.

Tell us not of banks and tariffs — cease your paltry
　　pedler cries —
Shall the good State sink her honor that your gam-
　　bling stocks may rise?
Would ye barter man for cotton? — That your gains
　　may be the same,

Must we kiss the feet of Moloch, pass our children
through the flame?
Is the dollar only real? — God and truth and right
a dream?
Weighed against your lying ledgers must our manhood kick the beam?

Oh, my God! — for that free spirit, which of old in
Boston town
Smote the Province House with terror, struck the
crest of Andros down! —
For another strong-voiced Adams in the city's streets
to cry:
"Up for God and Massachusetts! — Set your feet on
Mammon's lie!
Perish banks and perish traffic — spin your cotton's
latest pound —
But in Heaven's name keep your honor — keep the
heart o' the Bay State sound!"

Where's the MAN for Massachusetts? — Where's the
voice to speak her free? —
Where's the hand to light up bonfires from her
mountains to the sea?
Beats her Pilgrim pulse no longer? — Sits she dumb
in her despair? —
Has she none to break the silence? — Has she none
to do and dare?
Oh my God! for one right worthy to lift up her
rusted shield,
And to plant again the Pine Tree in her banner's
tattered field!

1846.

LINES

Suggested by a Visit to the City of Washington
in the 12th Month of 1845.

With a cold and wintry noon-light,
　　On its roofs and steeples shed,
Shadows weaving with the sun-light
　　From the gray sky overhead,
Broadly, vaguely, all around me, lies the half-built
　　town outspread.

Through this broad street, restless ever,
　　Ebbs and flows a human tide,
Wave on wave a living river;
　　Wealth and fashion side by side;
Toiler, idler, slave and master, in the same quick
　　current glide.

Underneath yon dome, whose coping
　　Springs above them, vast and tall,
Grave men in the dust are groping
　　For the largess, base and small,
Which the hand of Power is scattering, crumbs
　　which from its table fall.

Base of heart!　They vilely barter
　　Honor's wealth for party's place:
Step by step on Freedom's charter
　　Leaving footprints of disgrace;
For to-day's poor pittance turning from the great
　　hope of their race.

Yet, where festal lamps are throwing
   Glory round the dancer's hair,
Gold-tressed, like an angel's flowing
   Backward on the sunset air;
And the low quick pulse of music beats its measures
   sweet and rare:

There to-night shall woman's glances,
   Star-like, welcome give to them,
Fawning fools with shy advances
   Seek to touch their garments' hem,
With the tongue of flattery glozing deeds which God
   and Truth condemn.

From this glittering lie my vision
   Takes a broader, sadder range,
Full before me have arisen
   Other pictures dark and strange;
From the parlor to the prison must the scene and
   witness change.

Hark! the heavy gate is swinging
   On its hinges, harsh and slow;
One pale prison lamp is flinging
   On a fearful group below
Such a light as leaves to terror whatsoe'er it does
   not show.

Pitying God!—Is that a WOMAN
   On whose wrist the shackles clash?
Is that shriek she utters human,
   Underneath the stinging lash?

Are they MEN whose eyes of madness from that sad
    procession flash?

    Still the dance goes gayly onward!
      What is it to Wealth and Pride,
    That without the stars are looking
      On a scene which earth should hide?
That the SLAVE-SHIP lies in waiting, rocking on
    Potomac's tide!

    Vainly to that mean Ambition
      Which, upon a rival's fall,
    Winds above its old condition,
      With a reptile's slimy crawl,
Shall the pleading voice of sorrow, shall the slave in
    anguish call.

    Vainly to the child of Fashion,
      Giving to ideal woe
    Graceful luxury of compassion,
      Shall the stricken mourner go;
Hateful seems the earnest sorrow, beautiful the hol-
    low show!

    Nay, my words are all too sweeping:
      In this crowded human mart
    Feeling is not dead, but sleeping;
      Man's strong will and woman's heart,
In the coming strife for Freedom, yet shall bear their
    generous part.

    And from yonder sunny valleys,
      Southward in the distance lost,

Freedom yet shall summon allies
  Worthier than the North can boast,
With the Evil by their hearth-stones grappling at
    severer cost.

Now, the soul alone is willing:
  Faint the heart and weak the knee;
And as yet uo lip is thrilling
  With the mighty words " BE FREE!"
Tarrieth long the land's Good Angel, but his advent
    is to be!

Meanwhile, turning from the revel
  To the prison-cell my sight,
For intenser hate of evil,
  For a keener sense of right,
Shaking off thy dust, I thank thee, City of the Slaves,
    to-night!

"To thy duty now and ever!
  Dream no more of rest or stay;
Give to Freedom's great endeavor
  All thou art and hast to-day: " —
Thus, above the city's murmur, saith a Voice or
    seems to say.

Ye with heart and vision gifted
  To discern and love the right,
Whose worn faces have been lifted
  To the slowly-growing light,
Where from Freedom's sunrise drifted slowly back
    the murk of night! —

Ye who through long years of trial
　　Still have held your purpose fast,
While a lengthening shade the dial
　　From the westering sunshine cast,
And of hope each hour's denial seemed an echo of
　　the last! —

Oh, my brothers! oh, my sisters!
　　Would to God that ye were near,
Gazing with me down the vistas
　　Of a sorrow strange and drear;
Would to God that ye were listening to the Voice I
　　seem to hear!

With the storm above us driving,
　　With the false earth mined below —
Who shall marvel if thus striving
　　We have counted friend as foe;
Unto one another giving in the darkness blow for
　　blow?

Well it may be that our natures
　　Have grown sterner and more hard,
And the freshness of their features
　　Somewhat harsh and battle-scarred,
And their harmonies of feeling overtasked and rudely
　　jarred.

Be it so.　It should not swerve us
　　From a purpose true and brave;
Dearer Freedom's rugged service
　　Than the pastime of the slave:

Better is the storm above it than the quiet of the
  grave.

      Let us then, uniting, bury
        All our idle feuds in dust,
      And to future conflicts carry
        Mutual faith and common trust;
Always he who most forgiveth in his brother is most
  just.

      From the eternal shadow rounding
        All our sun and starlight here,
      Voices of our lost ones sounding
        Bid us be of heart and cheer,
Through the silence, down the spaces, falling on the
  inward ear.

      Know we not our dead are looking
        Downward with a sad surprise,
      All our strife of words rebuking
        With their mild and loving eyes?
Shall we grieve the holy angels? Shall we cloud their
  blessed skies?

      Let us draw their mantles o'er us
        Which have fallen in our way;
      Let us do the work before us,
        Cheerly, bravely, while we may,
Ere the long night-silence cometh, and with us it is
  not day!

  1845.

LINES

FROM A LETTER TO A YOUNG CLERICAL FRIEND.

A STRENGTH Thy service cannot tire —
   A faith which doubt can never dim —
A heart of love, a lip of fire —
   Oh! Freedom's God! be Thou to him!

Speak through him words of power and fear,
   As through Thy prophet bards of old,
And let a scornful people hear
   Once more Thy Sinai-thunders rolled.

For lying lips Thy blessing seek,
   And hands of blood are raised to Thee,
And on Thy children, crushed and weak,
   The oppressor plants his kneeling knee.

Let then, oh, God! Thy servant dare
   Thy truth in all its power to tell,
Unmask the priestly thieves, and tear
   The Bible from the grasp of hell!

From hollow rite and narrow span
   Of law and sect by Thee released,
Oh! teach him that the Christian man
   Is holier than the Jewish priest.

Chase back the shadows, gray and old,
　Of the dead ages from his way,
And let his hopeful eyes behold
　The dawn of Thy millennial day; —

That day when fettered limb and mind
　Shall know the truth which maketh free,
And he alone who loves his kind
　Shall, child-like, claim the love of Thee!

1846.

YORKTOWN.

[DR. THATCHER, surgeon in SCAMMEL'S regiment, in his description of the siege of Yorktown, says: "The labor on the Virginia plantations is performed altogether by a species of the human race cruelly wrested from their native country, and doomed to perpetual bondage, while their masters are manfully contending for freedom and the natural rights of man. Such is the inconsistency of human nature." Eighteen hundred slaves were found at Yorktown, after its surrender, and restored to their masters. Well was it said by DR. BARNES, in his late work on Slavery: "No slave was any nearer his freedom after the surrender of Yorktown, than when PATRICK HENRY first taught the notes of liberty to echo among the hills and vales of Virginia."]

FROM Yorktown's ruins, ranked and still,
Two lines stretch far o'er vale and hill:
Who curbs his steed at head of one?
Hark! the low murmur: Washington!
Who bends his keen, approving glance
Where down the gorgeous line of France

Shine knightly star and plume of snow?
Thou too art victor, Rochambeau!

The earth which bears this calm array
Shook with the war-charge yesterday,
Ploughed deep with hurrying hoof and wheel,
Shot-sown and bladed thick with steel;
October's clear and noonday sun
Paled in the breath-smoke of the gun,
And down night's double blackness fell,
Like a dropped star, the blazing shell.

Now all is hushed: the gleaming lines
Stand moveless as the neighboring pines;
While through them, sullen, grim, and slow
The conquered hosts of England go:
O'Hara's brow belies his dress,
Gay Tarlton's troop ride bannerless:
Shout, from thy fired and wasted homes,
Thy scourge, Virginia, captive comes!

Nor thou alone: with one glad voice
Let all thy sister States rejoice;
Let Freedom, in whatever clime
She waits with sleepless eye her time,
Shouting from cave and mountain wood,
Make glad her desert solitude,
While they who hunt her quail with fear:
The New World's chain lies broken here!

But who are they, who, cowering, wait
Within the shattered fortress gate?

Dark tillers of Virginia's soil,
Classed with the battle's common spoil,
With household stuffs, and fowl, and swine,
With Indian weed and planters' wine,
With stolen beeves, and foraged corn —
Are they not men, Virginian born ?

Oh! veil your faces, young and brave!
Sleep, Scammel, in thy soldier grave!
Sons of the North-land, ye who set
Stout hearts against the bayonet,
And pressed with steady footfall near
The moated battery's blazing tier,
Turn your scarred faces from the sight,
Let shame do homage to the right!

Lo! threescore years have passed; and where
The Gallic timbrel stirred the air,
With Northern drum-roll, and the clear,
Wild horn-blow of the mountaineer,
While Britain grounded on that plain
The arms she might not lift again,
As abject as in that old day
The slave still toils his life away.

Oh! fields still green and fresh in story,
Old days of pride, old names of glory,
Old marvels of the tongue and pen,
Old thoughts which stirred the hearts of men,
Ye spared the wrong; and over all
Behold the avenging shadow fall!
Your world-wide honor stained with shame —
Your freedom's self a hollow name!

Where's now the flag of that old war?
Where flows its stripe?   Where burns its star?
Bear witness, Palo Alto's day,
Dark Vale of Palms, red Monterey,
Where Mexic Freedom, young and weak,
Fleshes the Northern eagle's beak:
Symbol of terror and despair,
Of chains and slaves, go seek it there!

Laugh, Prussia, midst thy iron ranks!
Laugh, Russia, from thy Neva's banks!
Brave sport to see the fledgling born
Of Freedom by its parent torn!
Safe now is Spielberg's dungeon cell,
Safe drear Siberia's frozen hell:
With Slavery's flag o'er both unrolled,
What of the New World fears the Old?

1847.

EGO.

WRITTEN IN THE BOOK OF A FRIEND.

On page of thine I cannot trace
The cold and heartless common-place —
A statue's fixed and marble grace.

For ever as these lines are penned,
Still with the thought of thee will blend
That of some loved and common friend —

Who in life's desert track has made
His pilgrim tent with mine, or strayed
Beneath the same remembered shade.

And hence my pen unfettered moves
In freedom which the heart approves —
The negligence which friendship loves.

And wilt thou prize my poor gift less
For simple air and rustic dress,
And sign of haste and carelessness? —

Oh! more than specious counterfeit
Of sentiment, or studied wit,
A heart like thine should value it.

Yet half I fear my gift will be
Unto thy book, if not to thee,
Of more than doubtful courtesy.

A banished name from Fashion's sphere,
A lay unheard of Beauty's ear,
Forbid, disowned, — what do they here? —

Upon my ear not all in vain
Came the sad captive's clanking chain —
The groaning from his bed of pain.

And sadder still, I saw the woe
Which only wounded spirits know
When Pride's strong footsteps o'er them go.

Spurned not alone in walks abroad,
But from the "temples of the Lord"
Thrust out apart, like things abhorred.

Deep as I felt, and stern and strong,
In words which Prudence smothered long,
My soul spoke out against the wrong;

Not mine alone the task to speak
Of comfort to the poor and weak,
And dry the tear on Sorrow's cheek;

But, mingled in the conflict warm,
To pour the fiery breath of storm
Through the harsh trumpet of Reform;

To brave Opinion's settled frown,
From ermined robe and saintly gown,
While wrestling reverenced Error down.

Founts gushed beside my pilgrim way,
Cool shadows on the green sward lay,
Flowers swung upon the bending spray.

And, broad and bright, on either hand,
Stretched the green slopes of Fairy land,
With Hope's eternal sunbow spanned;

Whence voices called me like the flow,
Which on the listener's ear will grow,
Of forest streamlets soft and low.

And gentle eyes, which still retain
Their picture on the heart and brain,
Smiled, beckoning from that path of pain.

In vain! — nor dream, nor rest, nor pause
Remain for him who round him draws
The battered mail of Freedom's cause.

From youthful hopes — from each green spot
Of young Romance, and gentle Thought,
Where storm and tumult enter not —

From each fair altar, where belong
The offerings Love requires of Song
In homage to her bright-eyed throng —

With soul and strength, with heart and hand,
I turned to Freedom's struggling band —
To the sad Helots of our land.

What marvel then that Fame should turn
Her notes of praise to those of scorn —
Her gifts reclaimed — her smiles withdrawn?

What matters it! — a few years more,
Life's surge so restless heretofore
Shall break upon the unknown shore!

In that far land shall disappear
The shadows which we follow here —
The mist-wreaths of our atmosphere!

Before no work of mortal hand,
Of human will or strength expand
The pearl gates of the Better Land;

Alone in that great love which gave
Life to the sleeper of the grave,
Resteth the power to "seek and save."

Yet, if the spirit gazing through
The vista of the past can view
One deed to Heaven and virtue true —

If through the wreck of wasted powers,
Of garlands wreathed from Folly's bowers,
Of idle aims and misspent hours —

The eye can note one sacred spot
By Pride and Self profaned not —
A green place in the waste of thought —

Where deed or word has rendered less
"The sum of human wretchedness,"
And Gratitude looks forth to bless —

The simple burst of tenderest feeling
From sad hearts worn by evil-dealing,
For blessing on the hand of healing, —

Better than Glory's pomp will be
That green and blessed spot to me —
A palm-shade in Eternity! —

Something of Time which may invite
The purified and spiritual sight
To rest on with a calm delight.

And when the summer winds shall sweep
With their light wings my place of sleep,
And mosses round my head-stone creep —

If still, as Freedom's rallying sign,
Upon the young heart's altars shine
The very fires they caught from mine —

If words my lips once uttered still,
In the calm faith and steadfast will
Of other hearts, their work fulfil —

Perchance with joy the soul may learn
These tokens, and its eye discern
The fires which on those altars burn —

A marvellous joy that even then,
The spirit hath its life again,
In the strong hearts of mortal men.

Take, lady, then, the gift I bring,
No gay and graceful offering —
No flower-smile of the laughing spring.

Midst the green buds of Youth's fresh May,
With Fancy's leaf-enwoven bay,
My sad and sombre gift I lay.

And if it deepens in thy mind
A sense of suffering human kind —
The outcast and the spirit-blind:

Oppressed and spoiled on every side,
By Prejudice, and Scorn, and Pride,
Life's common courtesies denied;

Sad mothers mourning o'er their trust,
Children by want and misery nursed,
Tasting life's bitter cup at first;

If to their strong appeals which come
From the fireless hearth, and crowded room,
And the close alley's noisome gloom —

Though dark the hands upraised to thee
In mute beseeching agony,
Thou lend'st thy woman's sympathy —

Not vainly on thy gentle shrine,
Where Love, and Mirth, and Friendship twine
Their varied gifts, I offer mine.

1843.

MISCELLANEOUS.

THE FROST SPIRIT.

HE comes — he comes — the Frost Spirit comes!
    You may trace his footsteps now
On the naked woods and the blasted fields and the
    brown hill's withered brow.
He has smitten the leaves of the gray old trees
    where their pleasant green came forth,
And the winds, which follow wherever he goes, have
    shaken them down to earth.

He comes — he comes — the Frost Spirit comes! —
    from the frozen Labrador —
From the icy bridge of the Northern seas, which the
    white bear wanders o'er —
Where the fisherman's sail is stiff with ice, and the
    luckless forms below
In the sunless cold of the lingering night into marble
    statues grow!

He comes — he comes — the Frost Spirit comes! —
    on the rushing Northern blast,
And the dark Norwegian pines have bowed as his
    fearful breath went past.

With an unscorched wing he has hurried on, where
　　　the fires of Hecla glow
On the darkly beautiful sky above and the ancient ice
　　　below.

He comes — he comes — the Frost Spirit comes ! —
　　　and the quiet lake shall feel
The torpid touch of his glazing breath, and ring to
　　　the skater's heel ;
And the streams which danced on the broken rocks,
　　　or sang to the leaning grass,
Shall bow again to their winter chain, and in mourn-
　　　ful silence pass.

He comes — he comes — the Frost Spirit comes! —
　　　let us meet him as we may,
And turn with the light of the parlor-fire his evil
　　　power away ;
And gather closer the circle round, when that fire-
　　　light dances high,
And laugh at the shriek of the baffled Fiend as his
　　　sounding wing goes by!

　1830.

THE VAUDOIS TEACHER.

[" The manner in which the WALDENESES and heretics dis-
seminated their principles among the CATHOLIC gentry, was
by carrying with them a box of trinkets, or articles of dress.
Having entered the houses of the gentry, and disposed of some
of their goods, they cautiously intimated that they had com-

modities far more valuable than these — inestimable jewels, which they would show if they could be protected from the clergy. They would then give their purchasers a bible or testament; and thereby many were deluded into heresy."— *R. Saccho.*]

"OH, lady fair, these silks of mine are beautiful and rare —
The richest web of the Indian loom, which beauty's queen might wear;
And my pearls are pure as thine own fair neck, with whose radiant light they vie;
I have brought them with me a weary way, — will my gentle lady buy?"

And the lady smiled on the worn old man through the dark and clustering curls,
Which veiled her brow as she bent to view his silks and glittering pearls;
And she placed their price in the old man's hand, and lightly turned away,
But she paused at the wanderer's earnest call — "My gentle lady, stay!"

"Oh, lady fair, I have yet a gem which a purer lustre flings,
Than the diamond flash of the jewelled crown on the lofty brow of kings —
A wonderful pearl of exceeding price, whose virtue shall not decay,
Whose light shall be as a spell to thee and a blessing on thy way!"

The lady glanced at the mirroring steel where her
    form of grace was seen,
Where her eye shone clear, and her dark locks waved
    their clasping pearls between ; —
" Bring forth thy pearl of exceeding worth, thou
    traveller gray and old —
And name the price of thy precious gem, and my
    page shall count thy gold."

The cloud went off from the pilgrim's brow, as a
    small and meagre book,
Unchased with gold or gem of cost, from his folding
    robe he took!
" Here, lady fair, is the pearl of price, may it prove as
    such to thee!
Nay — keep thy gold — I ask it not, for the word of
    God is free! "

The hoary traveller went his way, but the gift he left
    behind
Hath had its pure and perfect work on that high-born
    maiden's mind,
And she hath turned from the pride of sin to the low-
    liness of truth,
And given her human heart to God in its beautiful
    hour of youth!

And she hath left the gray old halls, where an evil
    faith had power,
The courtly knights of her father's train, and the
    maidens of her power ;

And she hath gone to the Vaudois vales by lordly
    feet untrod,
Where the poor and needy of earth are rich in the
    perfect love of God!

   1830.

           —◦◦—

THE CALL OF THE CHRISTIAN.

Not always as the whirlwind's rush
  On Horeb's mount of fear,
Not always as the burning bush
  To Midian's shepherd seer,
Nor as the awful voice which came
  To Israel's prophet bards,
Nor as the tongues of cloven flame,
  Nor gift of fearful words —

Not always thus, with outward sign
  Of fire or voice from Heaven,
The message of a truth divine,
  The call of God is given!
Awaking in the human heart
  Love for the true and right —
Zeal for the Christian's " better part,"
  Strength for the Christian's fight.

Nor unto manhood's heart alone
  The holy influence steals :
Warm with a rapture not its own,
  The heart of woman feels!

As she who by Samaria's wall
   The Saviour's errand sought —
As those who with the fervent Paul
   And meek Aquila wrought:

Or those meek ones whose martydom
   Rome's gathered grandeur saw:
Or those who in their Alpine home
   Braved the Crusader's war,
When the green Vaudois, trembling, heard,
   Through all its vales of death,
The martyr's song of triumph poured
   From woman's failing breath.

And gently, by a thousand things
   Which o'er our spirits pass,
Like breezes o'er the harp's fine strings,
   Or vapors o'er a glass,
Leaving their token strange and new
   Of music or of shade,
The summons to the right and true
   And merciful is made.

Oh, then, if gleams of truth and light
   Flash o'er thy waiting mind,
Unfolding to thy mental sight
   The wants of human kind;
If brooding over human grief,
   The earnest wish is known
To soothe and gladden with relief
   An anguish not thine own:

Though heralded with naught of fear.
  Or outward sign, or show:
Though only to the inward ear
  It whispers soft and low;
Though dropping, as the manna fell,
  Unseen, yet from above,
Noiseless as dew-fall, heed it well —
  Thy Father's call of love!

1833.

MY SOUL AND I.

STAND still, my soul, in the silent dark
    I would question thee,
Alone in the shadow drear and stark
    With God and me!

What, my soul, was thy errand here?
    Was it mirth or ease,
Or heaping up dust from year to year?
    " Nay, none of these! "

Speak, soul, aright in His holy sight
    Whose eye looks still
And steadily on thee through the night:
    " To do His will! "

What hast thou done, oh soul of mine
    That thou tremblest so? —
Has thou wrought His task, and kept the line
    He bade thee go?

What, silent all !— art sad of cheer?
  Art fearful now?
When God seemed far and men were near
  How brave wert thou?

Aha! thou tremblest!— well I see
  Thou'rt craven grown.
Is it so hard with God and me
  To stand alone?—

Summon thy sunshine bravery back,
  Oh, wretched sprite!
Let me hear thy voice through this deep and black
  Abysmal night.

What hast thou wrought for Right and Truth,
  For God and Man,
From the golden hours of bright-eyed youth
  To life's mid span?

Ah, soul of mine, thy tones I hear,
  But weak and low,
Like far sad murmurs on my ear
  They come and go.

"I have wrestled stoutly with the Wrong,
  And borne the Right
From beneath the footfall of the throng
  To life and light.

" Wherever Freedom shivered a chain,
       God speed, quoth I ;
To Error amidst her shouting train
       I gave the lie."

Ah, soul of mine! ah, soul of mine!
       Thy deeds are well :
Were they wrought for Truth's sake or for thine?
       My soul, pray tell.

" Of all the work my hand hath wrought
       Beneath the sky,
Save a place in kindly human thought,
       No gain have I."

Go to, go to! — for thy very self
       Thy deeds were done :
Thou for fame, the miser for pelf
       Your end is one!

And where art thou going, soul of mine?
       Canst see the end?
And whither this troubled life of thine
       Evermore doth tend?

What daunts thee now? — what shakes thee so?
       My sad soul say.
" I see a cloud like a curtain low
       Hang o'er my way.

"Whither I go I cannot tell :
          That cloud hangs black,
High as the heaven and deep as hell,
          Across my track.

"I see its shadow coldly enwrap
          The souls before.
Sadly they enter it, step by step,
          To return no more.

"They shrink, they shudder, dear God! they kneel
          To Thee in prayer.
They shut their eyes on the cloud, but feel
          That it still is there.

"In vain they turn from the dread Before
          To the Known and Gone ;
For while gazing behind them evermore
          Their feet glide on.

"Yet, at times, I see upon sweet pale faces
          A light begin
To tremble, as if from holy places
          And shrines within.

"And at times methinks their cold lips move
          With hymn and prayer,
As if somewhat of awe, but more of love
          And hope were there.

"I call on the souls who have left the light
　　To reveal their lot;
I bend my ear to that wall of night,
　　And they answer not.

"But I hear around me sighs of pain
　　And the cry of fear,
And a sound like the slow sad dropping of rain,
　　Each drop a tear!

"Ah, the cloud is dark, and day by day,
　　I am moving thither:
I must pass beneath it on my way —
　　God pity me! — WHITHER?"

Ah soul of mine! so brave and wise
　　In the life-storm loud,
Fronting so calmly all human eyes
　　In the sun-lit crowd!

Now standing apart with God and me
　　Thou art weakness all,
Gazing vainly after the things to be
　　Through Death's dread wall.

But never for this, never for this
　　Was thy being lent;
For the craven's fear is but selfishness,
　　Like his merriment.

Folly and Fear are sisters twain:
    One closing her eyes,
The other peopling the dark inane
    With spectral lies.

Know well, my soul, God's hand controls
    Whate'er thou fearest;
Round Him in calmest music rolls
    Whate'er thou hearest.

What to thee is shadow, to Him is day,
    And the end He knoweth,
And not on a blind and aimless way
    The spirit goeth.

Man sees no future — a phantom show
    Is alone before him;
Past Time is dead, and the grasses grow,
    And flowers bloom o'er him.

Nothing before, nothing behind:
    The steps of Faith
Fall on the seeming void, and find
    The rock beneath.

The Present, the Present is all thou hast
    For thy sure possessing;
Like the patriarch's angel hold it fast
    Till it gives its blessing.

Why fear the night? why shrink from Death,
  That phantom wan?
There is nothing in Heaven or earth beneath
  Save God and man.

Peopling the shadows we turn from Him
  And from one another;
All is spectral and vague and dim
  Save God and our brother!

Like warp and woof all destinies
  Are woven fast,
Linked in sympathy like the keys
  Of an organ vast.

Pluck one thread, and the web ye mar;
  Break but one
Of a thousand keys, and the paining jar
  Through all will run.

Oh, restless spirit! wherefore strain
  Beyond thy sphere? —
Heaven and hell, with their joy and pain
  Are now and here.

Back to thyself is measured well
  All thou hast given;
Thy neighbor's wrong is thy present hell,
  His bliss thy heaven.

And in life, in death, in dark and light
     All are in God's care;
Sound the black abyss, pierce the deep of night,
     And He is there!

All which is real now remaineth,
     And fadeth never:
The hand which upholds it now, sustaineth
     The soul forever.

Leaning on Him, make with reverent meekness
     His own thy will,
And with strength from Him shall thy utter weakness
     Life's task fulfil;

And that cloud itself, which now before thee
     Lies dark in view,
Shall with beams of light from the inner glory
     Be stricken through.

And like meadow mist through Autumn's dawn
     Uprolling thin,
Its thickest folds when about thee drawn
     Let sunlight in.

Then of what is to be, and of what is done
     Why queriest thou? —
The past and the time to be are one,
     And both are NOW!

   1847.

TO A FRIEND,

On Her Return from Europe.

How smiled the land of France
Under thy blue eye's glance,
    Light-hearted rover!
Old walls of châteaux gray,
Towers of an early day,
Which the Three Colors play
    Flauntingly over.

Now midst the brilliant train
Thronging the banks of Seine:
    Now midst the splendor
Of the wild Alpine range,
Waking with change on change
Thoughts in thy young heart strange,
    Lovely, and tender.

Vales, soft Elysian,
Like those in the vision
    Of Mirza, when, dreaming,
He saw the long hollow dell,
Touched by the prophet's spell,
Into an ocean swell
    With its isles teeming.

Cliffs wrapped in snows of years,
Splintering with icy spears
    Autumn's blue heaven:

Loose rock and frozen slide,
Hung on the mountain side,
Waiting their hour to glide
      Downward, storm-driven!

Rhine stream, by castle old,
Baron's and robber's hold,
      Peacefully flowing;
Sweeping through vineyards green
Or where the cliffs are seen
O'er the broad wave between
      Grim shadows throwing.

Or where St. Peter's dome
Swells o'er eternal Rome,
      Vast, dim, and solemn, —
Hymns ever chanting low —
Censers swung to and fro —
Sable stoles sweeping slow
      Cornice and column!

Oh, as from each and all
Will there not voices call
      Evermore back again?
In the mind's gallery
Wilt thou not always see
Dim phantoms beckon thee
      O'er that old track again?

New forms thy presence haunt —
New voices softly chant —
      New faces greet thee! —

Pilgrims from many a shrine
Hallowed by poet's line,
At memory's magic sign,
    Rising to meet thee.

And when such visions come
Unto thy olden home,
    Will they not waken
Deep thoughts of Him whose hand
Led thee o'er sea and land
Back to the household band
    Whence thou wast taken?

While, at the sunset time,
Swells the cathedral's chime,
    Yet, in thy dreaming,
While to thy spirit's eye
Yet the vast mountains lie
Piled in the Switzer's sky,
    Icy and gleaming:

Prompter of silent prayer,
Be the wild picture there
    In the mind's chamber,
And, through each coming day
Him, who, as staff and stay,
Watched o'er thy wandering way,
    Freshly remember.

So, when the call shall be
Soon or late unto thee,
    As to all given,

> Still may that picture live,
> All its fair forms survive,
> And to thy spirit give
>   Gladness in Heaven!

1841.

———•◦•———

TO THE REFORMERS OF ENGLAND.[1]

> GOD bless ye, brothers! — in the fight
>   Ye're waging now, ye cannot fail,
> For better is your sense of right
>   Than kingcraft's triple mail.

> Than tyrant's law, or bigot's ban
>   More mighty is your simplest word;
> The free heart of an honest man
>   Than crosier or the sword.

> Go — let your bloated Church rehearse
>   The lesson it has learned so well;
> It moves not with its prayer or curse
>   The gates of Heaven or hell.

> Let the State scaffold rise again —
>   Did Freedom die when Russell died?
> Forget ye how the blood of Vane
>   From earth's green bosom cried?

[1] It can scarcely be necessary to say that the author refers to those who are seeking the reform of political evils in Great Britain by peaceful and Christian means.

The great hearts of your olden time
   Are beating with you, full and strong;
All holy memories and sublime
   And glorious round ye throng.

The bluff, bold men of Runnymede
   Are with ye still in times like these;
The shades of England's mighty dead,
   Your cloud of witnesses!

The truths ye urge are borne abroad
   By every wind and every tide;
The voice of Nature and of God
   Speaks out upon your side.

The weapons which your hands have found
   Are those which Heaven itself hath wrought,
Light, Truth, and Love; — your battle ground
   The free, broad field of Thought.

No partial, selfish purpose breaks
   The simple beauty of your plan,
Nor lie from throne or altar shakes
   Your steady faith in man.

The languid pulse of England starts
   And bounds beneath your words of power;
The beating of her million hearts
   Is with you at this hour!

Oh, ye who, with undoubting eyes,
    Through present cloud and gathering storm,
Behold the span of Freedom's skies,
    And sunshine soft and warm, —

Press bravely onward! — not in vain
    Your generous trust in human kind;
The good which bloodshed could not gain
    Your peaceful zeal shall find.

Press on! — the triumph shall be won
    Of common rights and equal laws,
The glorious dream of Harrington,
    And Sidney's good old cause.

Blessing the cotter and the crown,
    Sweetening worn Labor's bitter cup;
And, plucking not the highest down,
    Lifting the lowest up.

Press on! — and we who may not share
    The toil or glory of your fight,
May ask, at least, in earnest prayer,
    God's blessing on the right!

1843.

THE QUAKER OF THE OLDEN TIME.

THE Quaker of the olden time! —
    How calm and firm and true,
Unspotted by its wrong and crime,
    He walked the dark earth through!

The lust of power, the love of gain,
　The thousand lures of sin
Around him, had no power to stain
　The purity within.

With that deep insight which detects
　All great things in the small,
And knows how each man's life affects
　The spiritual life of all,
He walked by faith and not by sight,
　By love and not by law;
The presence of the wrong or right
　He rather felt than saw.

He felt that wrong with wrong partakes,
　That nothing stands alone,
That whoso gives the motive, makes
　His brother's sin his own.
And, pausing not for doubtful choice
　Of evils great or small,
He listened to that inward voice
　Which called away from all.

Oh! Spirit of that early day,
　So pure and strong and true,
Be with us in the narrow way
　Our faithful fathers knew.
Give strength the evil to forsake,
　The cross of Truth to bear,
And love and reverent fear to make
　Our daily lives a prayer!

1838.

THE REFORMER.

ALL grim and soiled and brown with tan,
    I saw a Strong One, in his wrath,
Smiting the godless shrines of man
        Along his path.

The Church beneath her trembling dome
    Essayed in vain her ghostly charm:
Wealth shook within his gilded home
        With strange alarm.

Fraud from his secret chambers fled
    Before the sunlight bursting in;
Sloth drew her pillow o'er her head
        To drown the din.

" Spare," Art implored, " yon holy pile;
    That grand, old, time-worn, turret spare · "
Meek Reverence, kneeling in the aisle,
        Cried out, " Forbear! "

Gray-bearded Use, who, deaf and blind,
    Groped for his old accustomed stone,
Leaned on his staff, and wept, to find
        His seat o'erthrown.

Young Romance raised his dreamy eyes,
    O'erhung with paly locks of gold:
" Why smite," he asked in sad surprise,
        " The fair, the old? "

Yet louder rang the Strong One's stroke,
　　Yet nearer flashed his axe's gleam;
Shuddering and sick at heart I woke,
　　　　As from a dream.

I looked: aside the dust cloud rolled —
　　The Waster seemed the Builder too;
Upspringing from the ruined Old
　　　　I saw the New.

'T was but the ruin of the bad —
　　The wasting of the wrong and ill;
Whate'er of good the old time had
　　　　Was living still.

Calm grew the brows of him I feared;
　　The frown which awed me passed away,
And left behind a smile which cheered
　　　　Like breaking day.

The grain grew green on battle-plains,
　　O'er swarded war-mounds grazed the cow;
The slave stood forging from his chains
　　　　The spade and plough.

Where frowned the fort, pavilions gay
　　And cottage windows, flower-entwined,
Looked out upon the peaceful bay
　　　　And hills behind.

Through vine-wreathed cups with wine once red,
   The lights on brimming crystal fell,
Drawn, sparkling, from the rivulet head
     And mossy well.

Through prison walls, like Heaven-sent hope,
   Fresh breezes blew, and sunbeams strayed,
And with the idle gallows-rope
     The young child played.

Where the doomed victim in his cell
   Had counted o'er the weary hours,
Glad school-girls, answering to the bell,
     Came crowned with flowers.

Grown wiser for the lesson given,
   I fear no longer, for I know
That, where the share is deepest driven,
     The best fruits grow.

The outworn rite, the old abuse,
   The pious fraud transparent grown,
The good held captive in the use
     Of wrong alone —

These wait their doom, from that great law
   Which makes the past time serve to-day;
And fresher life the world shall draw
     From their decay.

Oh! backward-looking son of time! —
    The new is old, the old is new,
The cycle of a change sublime
        Still sweeping through.

So wisely taught the Indian seer;
    Destroying Seva, forming Brahm,
Who wake by turns Earth's love and fear,
        Are one, the same.

As idly as, in that old day
    Thou mournest, did thy sires repine,
So, in his time, thy child, grown gray,
        Shall sigh for thine.

Yet, not the less for them or thou
    The eternal step of Progress beats
To that great anthem, calm and slow,
        Which God repeats!

Take heart! — the Waster builds again —
    A charmed life old goodness hath;
The tares may perish — but the grain
        Is not for death.

God works in all things; all obey
    His first propulsion from the night:
Ho, wake and watch! — the world is gray
        With morning light!

1846.

THE PRISONER FOR DEBT.

LOOK on him! — through his dungeon grate
　　Feebly and cold, the morning light
Comes stealing round him, dim and late,
　　As if it loathed the sight.
Reclining on his strawy bed,
His hand upholds his drooping head —
His bloodless cheek is seamed and hard,
Unshorn his gray, neglected beard;
And o'er his bony fingers flow
His long, dishevelled locks of snow.

No grateful fire before him glows,
　　And yet the winter's breath is chill;
And o'er his half-clad person goes
　　The frequent ague thrill!
Silent, save ever and anon,
A sound, half murmur and half groan,
Forces apart the painful grip
Of the old sufferer's bearded lip;
O sad and crushing is the fate
Of old age chained and desolate!

Just God! why lies that old man there?
　　A murderer shares his prison bed,
Whose eye-balls, through his horrid hair,
　　Gleam on him, fierce and red;
And the rude oath and heartless jeer
Fall ever on his loathing ear,

And, or in wakefulness or sleep,
Nerve, flesh, and pulses thrill and creep
Whene'er that ruffian's tossing limb,
Crimson with murder, touches him!

What has the gray-haired prisoner done?
  Has murder stained his hands with gore?
Not so; his crime's a fouler one;
  GOD MADE THE OLD MAN POOR!
For this he shares a felon's cell —
The fittest earthly type of hell!
For this, the boon for which he poured
His young blood on the invader's sword,
And counted light the fearful cost —
His blood-gained liberty is lost!

And so, for such a place of rest,
  Old prisoner, dropped thy blood as rain
On Concord's field, and Bunker's crest,
  And Saratoga's plain?
Look forth, thou man of many scars,
Through thy dim dungeon's iron bars;
It must be joy, in sooth, to see
Yon monument upreared to thee —
Piled granite and a prison cell —
The land repays thy service well!

Go, ring the bells and fire the guns,
  And fling the starry banner out;
Shout "Freedom!" till your lisping ones
  Give back their cradle-shout:

Let boastful eloquence declaim
Of honor, liberty, and fame;
Still let the poet's strain be heard,
With glory for each second word,
And everything with breath agree
To praise " our glorious liberty ! "

But when the patriot cannon jars
    That prison's cold and gloomy wall,
And through its grates the stripes and stars
    Rise on the wind and fall —
Think ye that prisoner's aged ear
Rejoices in the general cheer?
Think ye his dim and failing eye
Is kindled at your pageantry?
Sorrowing of soul, and chained of limb,
What is your carnival to him?

Down with the LAW that binds him thus!
    Unworthy freemen, let it find
No refuge from the withering curse
    Of God and human kind!
Open the prison's living tomb,
And usher from its brooding gloom
The victims of your savage code,
To the free sun and air of God;
No longer dare as crime to brand
The chastening of the Almighty's hand.

1847.

LINES,

WRITTEN ON READING SEVERAL PAMPHLETS PUBLISHED
BY CLERGYMEN AGAINST THE ABOLITION OF THE
GALLOWS.

I.

THE suns of eighteen centuries have shone
   Since the Redeemer walked with man, and made
The fisher's boat, the cavern's floor of stone,
   And mountain moss, a pillow for his head;
And He, who wandered with the peasant Jew,
   And broke with publicans the bread of shame,
   And drank, with blessings in His Father's name,
The water which Samaria's outcast drew,
Hath now His temples upon every shore,
   Altar and shrine and priest, — and incense dim
   Evermore rising, with low prayer and hymn,
From lips which press the temple's marble floor,
Or kiss the gilded sign of the dread Cross He bore!

II.

Yet as of old, when, meekly "doing good,"
He fed a blind and selfish multitude,
And even the poor companions of His lot
With their dim earthly vision knew Him not,
   How ill are His high teachings understood!
Where He hath spoken Liberty, the priest
   At His own altar binds the chain anew;
Where He hath bidden to Life's equal feast,
   The starving many wait upon the few;

Where He hath spoken Peace, His name hath been
The loudest war-cry of contending men;
Priests, pale with vigils, in His name have blessed
The unsheathed sword, and laid the spear in rest,
Wet the war-banner with their sacred wine,
And crossed its blazon with the holy sign;
Yea, in His name who bade the erring live,
And daily taught His lesson — to forgive! —
   Twisted the cord and edged the murderous steel;
And, with His words of mercy on their lips,
Hung gloating o'er the pincer's burning grips,
   And the grim horror of the straining wheel;
Fed the slow flame which gnawed the victim's limb,
Who saw before his searing eye-balls swim
   The image of *their* Christ, in cruel zeal,
Through the black torment-smoke, held mockingly
     to him!

III.

The blood which mingled with the desert sand,
   And beaded with its red and ghastly dew
The vines and olives of the Holy Land —
   The shrieking curses of the hunted Jew —
The white-sown bones of heretics, where'er
They sank beneath the Crusade's holy spear —
Goa's dark dungeons — Malta's sea-washed cell,
   Where with the hymns the ghostly fathers sung
   Mingled the groans by subtle torture wrung,
Heaven's anthem blending with the shriek of hell!
The midnight of Bartholomew — the stake
   Of Smithfield, and that thrice-accursed flame
Which Calvin kindled by Geneva's lake —

New England's scaffold, and the priestly sneer
Which mocked its victims in that hour of fear,
  When guilt itself a human tear might claim, —
Bear witness, O Thou wronged and merciful One!
That Earth's most hateful crimes have in Thy name
      been done!

IV.

Thank God! that I have lived to see the time
  When the great truth begins at last to find
  An utterance from the deep heart of mankind,
Earnest and clear, that ALL REVENGE IS CRIME!
That man is holier than a creed, — that all
  Restraint upon him must consult his good,
Hope's sunshine linger on his prison wall,
  And Love look in upon his solitude.
The beautiful lesson which our Saviour taught
Through long, dark centuries its way hath wrought
Into the common mind and popular thought;
And words, to which by Galilee's lake shore
The humble fishers listened with hushed oar,
Have found an echo in the general heart,
And of the public faith become a living part.

V.

Who shall arrest this tendency? — Bring back
The cells of Venice and the bigot's rack?
Harden the softening human heart again
To cold indifference to a brother's pain?
Ye most unhappy men! — who, turned away,
From the mild sunshine of the Gospel day,
  Grope in the shadows of Man's twilight time,

What mean ye, that with ghoul-like zest ye brood
O'er those foul altars streaming with warm blood,
　　Permitted in another age and clime?
Why cite that law with which the bigot Jew
Rebuked the Pagan's mercy, when he knew
No evil in the Just One? — Wherefore turn
To the dark cruel past? — Can we not learn
From the pure Teacher's life, how mildly free
Is the great Gospel of Humanity?
The Flamen's knife is bloodless, and no more
Mexitli's altars soak with human gore,
No more the ghastly sacrifices smoke
Through the green arches of the Druid's oak;
And ye of milder faith, with your high claim
Of prophet-utterance in the Holiest name,
Will ye become the Druids of *our* time?
　　Set up your scaffold-altars in *our* land,
And, consecrators of Law's darkest clime,
　　Urge to its loathsome work the hangman's hand?
Beware — lest human nature, roused at last,
From its peeled shoulder your encumbrance cast,
　　And, sick to loathing of your cry for blood,
Rank ye with those who led their victims round
The Celt's red altar and the Indian's mound,
　　Abhorred of Earth and Heaven — a pagan brother-
　　　　hood!

　1842.

THE HUMAN SACRIFICE.[1]

I.

FAR from his close and noisome cell,
  By grassy lane and sunny stream,
Blown clover field and strawberry dell,
And green and meadow freshness, fell
  The footsteps of his dream.
Again from careless feet the dew
  Of summer's misty morn he shook;
Again with merry heart he threw
  His light line in the rippling brook.
Back crowded all his school-day joys —
  He urged the ball and quoit again,
And heard the shout of laughing boys
  Come ringing down the walnut glen.
Again he felt the western breeze,
  With scent of flowers and crisping hay;
And down again through wind-stirred trees
  He saw the quivering sunlight play.
An angel in home's vine-hung door,
He saw his sister smile once more;
Once more the truant's brown-locked head
Upon his mother's knee was laid,
And sweetly lulled to slumber there,
With evening's holy hymn and prayer.

[1] Some of the leading sectarian papers have lately published the letter of a clergyman, giving an account of his attendance upon a criminal (who had committed murder during a fit of intoxication), at the time of his execution, in western New York.

II.

He woke.   At once on heart and brain
The present Terror rushed again —
Clanked on his limbs the felon's chain!
He woke, to hear the church-tower tell
Time's foot-fall on the conscious bell,
And, shuddering, feel that clanging din
His life's LAST HOUR had ushered in;
To see within his prison yard,
Through the small window, iron-barred,
The gallows' shadow rising dim
Between the sunrise heaven and him, —
A horror in God's blessed air —
   A blackness in His morning light —
Like some foul devil-altar there
   Built up by demon hands at night.
   And, maddened by that evil sight,
Dark, horrible, confused, and strange,
A chaos of wild, weltering change,
All power of check and guidance gone,
Dizzy and blind, his mind swept on.
In vain he strove to breathe a prayer,
   In vain he turned the Holy Book;
He only heard the gallows-stair
   Creak as the wind its timbers shook.

The writer describes the agony of the wretched being — his
abortive attempts at prayer — his appeal for life — his fear of a
violent death; and, after declaring his belief that the poor victim died without hope of salvation, concludes with a warm
eulogy upon the Gallows, being more than ever convinced of
its utility by the awful dread and horror which it inspired.

No dream for him of sin forgiven,
　　While still that baleful spectre stood,
　　With its hoarse murmur, "*Blood for blood!*"
Between him and the pitying Heaven!

III.

Low on his dungeon floor he knelt,
　　And smote his breast, and on his chain,
Whose iron clasp he always felt,
　　His hot tears fell like rain;
And near him, with the cold, calm look
　　And tone of one whose formal part,
　　Unwarmed, unsoftened of the heart,
Is measured out by rule and book,
With placid lip and tranquil blood,
The hangman's ghostly ally stood,
Blessing with solemn text and word
The gallows-drop and strangling cord;
Lending the sacred Gospel's awe
And sanction to the crime of Law.

IV.

He saw the victim's tortured brow —
　　The sweat of anguish starting there —
The record of a nameless woe
　　In the dim eye's imploring stare,
　　Seen hideous through the long, damp hair —
Fingers of ghastly skin and bone
Working and writhing on the stone! —
And heard, by mortal terror wrung
From heaving breast and stiffened tongue,
　　The choking sob and low hoarse prayer;

As o'er his half-crazed fancy came
A vision of the eternal flame —
Its smoking cloud of agonies —
Its demon-worm that never dies —
The everlasting rise and fall
Of fire-waves round the infernal wall;
While high above that dark red flood,
Black, giant-like, the gallows stood:
Two busy fiends attending there;
One with cold mocking rite and prayer,
The other, with impatient grasp,
Tightening the death-rope's strangling clasp!

v.

The unfelt rite at length was done —
  The prayer unheard at length was said —
An hour had passed : — the noon-day sun
  Smote on the features of the dead!
And he who stood the doomed beside,
Calm gauger of the swelling tide
Of mortal agony and fear,
Heeding with curious eye and ear
Whate'er revealed the keen excess
Of man's extremest wretchedness :
And who in that dark anguish saw
  An earnest of the victim's fate,
The vengeful terrors of God's law,
  The kindlings of Eternal hate —
The first drops of that fiery rain
Which beats the dark red realm of pain, —
Did he uplift his earnest cries
  Against the crime of Law, which gave
  His brother to that fearful grave,

Whereon Hope's moonlight never lies,
  And Faith's white blossoms never wave
To the soft breath of Memory's sighs ; —
Which sent a spirit marred and stained,
By fiends of sin possessed, profaned,
In madness and in blindness stark,
Into the silent, unknown dark?
No — from the wild and shrinking dread
With which he saw the victim led
  Beneath the dark veil which divides
Ever the living from the dead,
  And Nature's solemn secret hides,
The man of prayer can only draw
New reasons for his bloody law ;
New faith in staying Murder's hand
By murder at that Law's command ;
New reverence for the gallows-rope,
As human nature's latest hope ;
Last relic of the good old time,
When Power found license for its crime,
And held a writhing world in check
By that fell cord about its neck ;
Stifled Sedition's rising shout,
Choked the young breath of Freedom out,
And timely checked the words which sprung
From Heresy's forbidden tongue ;
While in its noose of terror bound,
The Church its cherished union found,
Conforming, on the Moslem plan,
The motley-colored mind of man,
Not by the Koran and the Sword,
But by the Bible and the Cord!

VI.

Oh, Thou! at whose rebuke the grave
Back to warm life its sleeper gave,
Beneath whose sad and tearful glance
The cold and changed countenance
Broke the still horror of its trance,
And waking, saw with joy above,
A brother's face of tenderest love;
Thou, unto whom the blind and lame,
The sorrowing and the sin-sick came,
And from thy very garment's hem
Drew life and healing unto them,
The burden of Thy holy faith
Was love and life, not hate and death,
Man's demon-ministers of pain,
　　The fiends of his revenge, were sent
　　From Thy pure Gospel's element
To their dark home again.
Thy name is Love! What, then, is he,
　　Who in that name the gallows rears,
An awful altar built to Thee,
　　With sacrifice of blood and tears?
Oh, once again Thy healing lay
　　On the blind eyes which know Thee not;
And let the light of Thy pure day
　　Melt in upon his darkened thought.
Soften his hard, cold heart, and show
　　The power which in forbearance lies,
And let him feel that mercy now
　　Is better than old sacrifice!

VII.

As on the White Sea's [1] charmed shore,
  The Parsee sees his holy hill
With dunnest smoke-clouds curtained o'er,
Yet knows beneath them, evermore,
  The low, pale fire is quivering still;
So underneath its clouds of sin,
  The heart of man retaineth yet
Gleams of its holy origin;
  And half-quenched stars that never set,
Dim colors of its faded bow,
  And early beauty, linger there,
And o'er its wasted desert blow
  Faint breathings of its morning air.
Oh! never yet upon the scroll
Of the sin-stained, but priceless soul,
  Hath Heaven inscribed " DESPAIR!"
Cast not the clouded gem away,
Quench not the dim but living ray—
  My brother man, Beware!
With that deep voice which from the skies
Forbade the Patriarch's sacrifice,
  God's angel cries, FORBEAR!

1843.

[1] Among the Tartars, the Caspian is known as *Akdingis*,
that is, White Sea. Baku, on its Persian side, is remarkable
for its perpetual fire, scarcely discoverable under the pitchy
clouds of smoke from the bitumen which feeds it. It is the
natural fire-altar of the old Persian worship.

RANDOLPH OF ROANOKE.

OH, Mother Earth! upon thy lap
  Thy weary ones receiving,
And o'er them, silent as a dream,
  Thy grassy mantle weaving,
Fold softly in thy long embrace
  That heart so worn and broken,
And cool its pulse of fire beneath
  Thy shadows old and oaken.

Shut out from him the bitter word
  And serpent hiss of scorning;
Nor let the storms of yesterday
  Disturb his quiet morning.
Breathe over him forgetfulness
  Of all save deeds of kindness,
And, save to smiles of grateful eyes,
  Press down his lids in blindness.

There, where with living ear and eye
  He heard Potomac's flowing,
And, through his tall ancestral trees,
  Saw autumn's sunset glowing,
He sleeps — still looking to the West,
  Beneath the dark wood shadow,
As if he still would see the sun
  Sink down on wave and meadow.

Bard, Sage, and Tribune! — in himself
  All moods of mind contrasting —

The tenderest wail of human woe,
   The scorn like lightning blasting;
The pathos which from rival eyes
   Unwilling tears could summon,
The stinging taunt, the fiery burst
   Of hatred scarcely human!

Mirth, sparkling like a diamond shower,
   From lips of life-long sadness;
Clear picturings of majestic thought
   Upon a ground of madness;
And over all Romance and Song
   A classic beauty throwing,
And laurelled Clio at his side
   Her storied pages showing.

All parties feared him: each in turn
   Beheld its schemes disjointed,
As right or left his fatal glance
   And spectral finger pointed.
Sworn foe of Cant, he smote it down
   With trenchant wit unsparing,
And, mocking, rent with ruthless hand
   The robe Pretence was wearing.

Too honest or too proud to feign
   A love he never cherished,
Beyond Virginia's border line
   His patriotism perished.
While others hailed in distant skies
   Our eagle's dusky pinion,
He only saw the mountain bird
   Stoop o'er his Old Dominion!

Still through each change of fortune strange,
 Racked nerve, and brain all burning,
His loving faith in Mother-land
 Knew never shade of turning;
By Britain's lakes, by Neva's wave,
 Whatever sky was o'er him,
He heard her rivers' rushing sound,
 Her blue peaks rose before him.

He held his slaves, yet made withal
 No false and vain pretences,
Nor paid a lying priest to seek
 For scriptural defences.
His harshest words of proud rebuke,
 His bitterest taunt and scorning,
Fell fire-like on the Northern brow
 That bent to him in fawning.

He held his slaves: yet kept the while
 His reverence for the Human;
In the dark vassals of his will
 He saw but Man and Woman!
No hunter of God's outraged poor
 His Roanoke valley entered;
No trader in the souls of men
 Across his threshold ventured.[1]

And when the old and wearied man
 Laid down for his last sleeping,

---

[1] Randolph had a hearty hatred of slave traders, and it is said treated some of them quite roughly, who ventured to cheapen his "chattels personal."

And at his side, a slave no more,
　　His brother man stood weeping,
His latest thought, his latest breath,
　　To Freedom's duty giving,
With failing tongue and trembling hand
　　The dying blest the living.

Oh! never bore his ancient State
　　A truer son or braver!
None trampling with a calmer scorn
　　On foreign hate or favor.
He knew her faults, yet never stooped
　　His proud and manly feeling
To poor excuses of the wrong
　　Or meanness of concealing.

But none beheld with clearer eye
　　The plague-spot o'er her spreading,
None heard more sure the steps of Doom
　　Along her future treading.
For her as for himself he spake,
　　When, his gaunt frame upbracing,
He traced with dying hand " REMORSE! " [1]
　　And perished in the tracing.

As from the grave where Henry sleeps,
　　From Vernon's weeping willow,
And from the grassy pall which hides
　　The Sage of Monticello,

[1] See the remarkable statement of Dr. Parish, his medical
attendant.

So from the leaf-strewn burial-stone
    Of Randolph's lowly dwelling,
Virginia! o'er thy land of slaves
    A warning voice is swelling!

And hark! from thy deserted fields
    Are sadder warnings spoken,
From quenched hearths, where thy exiled sons
    Their household gods have broken.
The curse is on thee — wolves for men,
    And briars for corn-sheaves giving!
Oh! more than all thy dead renown
    Were now one hero living!

1847.

DEMOCRACY.

["All things whatsoever ye would that men should do to
you, do ye even so to them." — *Matthew* vii. 12.]

BEARER of Freedom's holy light,
    Breaker of Slavery's chain and rod,
The foe of all which pains the light,
    Or wounds the generous ear of God!

Beautiful yet thy temples rise,
    Though there profaning gifts are thrown;
And fires unkindled of the skies
    Are glaring round thy altar-stone.

Still sacred — though thy name be breathed
  By those whose hearts thy truth deride;
And garlands, plucked from thee, are wreathed
  Around the haughty brows of Pride.

O, ideal of my boyhood's time!
  The faith in which my father stood,
Even when the sons of Lust and Crime
  Had stained thy peaceful courts with blood!

Still to those courts my footsteps turn.
  For through the mists which darken there,
I see the flame of Freedom burn —
  The Kebla of the patriot's prayer!

The generous feeling, pure and warm,
  Which owns the rights of *all* divine —
The pitying heart — the helping arm —
  The prompt self-sacrifice — are thine.

Beneath thy broad, impartial eye,
  How fade the lines of caste and birth!
How equal in their suffering lie
  The groaning multitudes of earth!

Still to a stricken brother true,
  Whatever clime hath nurtured him;
As stooped to heal the wounded Jew
  The worshipper of Gerizim.

By misery unrepelled, unawed
  By pomp or power, thou seest a MAN
In prince or peasant — slave or lord —
  Pale priest, or swarthy artisan.

Through all disguise, form, place, or name,
  Beneath the flaunting robes of sin,
Through poverty and squalid shame,
  Thou lookest on *the man* within.

On man, as man, retaining yet,
  Howe'er debased, and soiled, and dim,
The crown upon his forehead set —
  The immortal gift of God to him.

And there is reverence in thy look ;
  For that frail form which mortals wear
The Spirit of the Holiest took,
  And veiled His perfect brightness there.

Not from the shallow babbling fount
  Of vain philosophy thou art ;
He who of old on Syria's mount
  Thrilled, warmed, by turns, the listener's heart,

In holy words which cannot die,
  In thoughts which angels leaned to know,
Proclaimed thy message from on high —
  Thy mission to a world of woe.

That voice's echo hath not died!
    From the blue lake of Galilee,
And Tabor's lonely mountain side,
    It calls a struggling world to thee.

Thy name and watchword o'er this land
    I hear in every breeze that stirs,
And round a thousand altars stand
    Thy banded party worshippers.

Not to these altars of a day,
    At party's call, my gift I bring;
But on thy olden shrine I lay
    A freeman's dearest offering: —

The voiceless utterance of his will —
    His pledge to Freedom and to Truth,
That manhood's heart remembers still
    The homage of his generous youth.

Election Day, 1843.

———◦✦◦———

TO RONGE.

STRIKE home, strong-hearted man!   Down to the
        root
Of old oppression sink the Saxon steel.
Thy work is to hew down.   In God's name then
Put nerve into thy task.   Let other men
Plant, as they may, that better tree, whose fruit
The wounded bosom of the Church shall heal.
Be thou the image-breaker.   Let thy blows
Fall heavy as the Suabian's iron hand,

On crown or crosier, which shall interpose
Between thee and the weal of Father-land.
Leave creeds to closet idlers.   First of all,
Shake thou all German dream-land with the fall
Of that accursed tree, whose evil trunk
Was spared of old by Erfurt's stalwart monk.
Fight not with ghosts and shadows.   Let us hear
The snap of chain-links.   Let our gladdened ear
Catch the pale prisoner's welcome, as the light
Follows thy axe-stroke, through his cell of night.
Be faithful to both worlds; nor think to feed
Earth's starving millions with the husks of creed.
Servant of Him whose mission high and holy
Was to the wronged, the sorrowing, and the lowly,
Thrust not His Eden promise from our sphere,
Distant and dim beyond the blue sky's span;
Like him of Patmos, see it, now and here, —
The New Jerusalem comes down to man!
Be warned by Luther's error.   Nor like him,
When the roused Teuton dashes from his limb
The rusted chain of ages, help to bind
His hands, for whom thou claim'st the freedom of
          the mind!

1846.

CHALKLEY HALL.[1]

How bland and sweet the greeting of this breeze
    To him who flies
From crowded street and red wall's weary gleam,
Till far behind him like a hideous dream
    The close dark city lies! —

Here, while the market murmurs, while men throng
    The marble floor
Of Mammon's altar, from the crush and din
Of the world's madness let me gather in
    My better thoughts once more.

Oh! once again revive, while on my ear
    The cry of Gain
And low hoarse hum of Traffic dies away,
Ye blessed memories of my early day
    Like sere grass wet with rain! —

---

[1] Chalkley Hall, near Frankford, Pa., the residence of THOMAS CHALKLEY, an eminent minister of the "Friends" denomination. He was one of the early settlers of the Colony, and his Journal, which was published in 1749, presents a quaint but beautiful picture of a life of unostentatious and simple goodness. He was the master of a merchant vessel, and, in his visits to the West Indies and Great Britain, omitted no opportunity to labor for the highest interests of his fellow-men. During a temporary residence in Philadelphia, in the summer of 1838, the quiet and beautiful scenery around the ancient village of Frankford frequently attracted me from the heat and bustle of the city.

Once more let God's green earth and sunset air
    Old feelings waken ;
Through weary years of toil and strife and ill,
Oh, let me feel that my good angel still
    Hath not his trust forsaken.

And well do time and place befit my mood :
    Beneath the arms
Of this embracing wood, a good man made
His home, like Abraham resting in the shade
    Of Mamre's lonely palms.

Here, rich with autumn gifts of countless years,
    The virgin soil
Turned from the share he guided, and in rain
And summer sunshine throve the fruits and grain
    Which blessed his honest toil.

Here, from his voyages on the stormy seas,
    Weary and worn,
He came to meet his children, and to bless
The Giver of all good in thankfulness
    And praise for his return.

And here his neighbors gathered in to greet
    Their friend again,
Safe from the wave and the destroying gales,
Which reap untimely green Bermuda's vales,
    And vex the Carib main.

To hear the good man tell of simple truth,
    Sown in an hour
Of weakness in some far-off Indian isle,

From the parched bosom of a barren soil,
    Raised up in life and power:

How at those gatherings in Barbadian vales,
    A tendering love
Came o'er him, like the gentle rain from heaven,
And words of fitness to his lips were given,
    And strength as from above:

How the sad captive listened to the Word,
    Until his chain
Grew lighter, and his wounded spirit felt
The healing balm of consolation melt
    Upon its life-long pain:

How the armed warrior sate him down to hear
    Of Peace and Truth,
And the proud ruler and his Creole dame,
Jewelled and gorgeous in her beauty came,
    And fair and bright-eyed youth.

Oh, far away beneath New England's sky,
    Even when a boy,
Following my plough by Merrimack's green shore,
His simple record I have pondered o'er
    With deep and quiet joy.

And hence this scene, in sunset glory warm —
    Its woods around,
Its still stream winding on in light and shade,
Its soft, green meadows and its upland glade —
    To me is holy ground.

And dearer far than haunts where Genius keeps
　　His vigils still;
Than that where Avon's son of song is laid,
Or Vaucluse hallowed by its Petrarch's shade,
　　Or Virgil's laurelled hill.

To the gray walls of fallen Paraclete,
　　To Juliet's urn,
Fair Arno and Sorrento's orange grove,
Where Tasso sang, let young Romance and Love
　　Like brother pilgrims turn.

But here a deeper and serener charm
　　To all is given;
And blessed memories of the faithful dead
O'er wood and vale and meadow-stream have shed
　　The holy hues of Heaven!

　　1843.

———◦◦———

TO JOHN PIERPONT.

NOT as a poor requital of the joy
　　With which my childhood heard that lay of thine,
　　Which, like an echo of the song divine
At Bethlehem breathed above the Holy Boy,
　　Bore to my ear the airs of Palestine, —
Not to the poet, but the man I bring
In friendship's fearless trust my offering:
How much it lacks I feel, and thou wilt see,
Yet well I know that thou hast deemed with me

Life all too earnest, and its time too short
For dreamy ease and Fancy's graceful sport;
  And girded for thy constant strife with wrong,
Like Nehemiah fighting while he wrought
  The broken walls of Zion, even thy song
Hath a rude martial tone, a blow in every thought!

  1843.

THE CYPRESS TREE OF CEYLON.

[Ibn Batuta, the celebrated Mussulman traveller of the four-
teenth century, speaks of a Cypress tree in Ceylon, universally
held sacred by the natives, the leaves of which were said to fall
only at certain intervals, and he who had the happiness to find
and eat one of them, was restored, at once, to youth and vigor.
The traveller saw several venerable JOGEES, or saints, sitting
silent and motionless under the tree, patiently awaiting the falling of a leaf.]

  THEY sat in silent watchfulness
    The sacred cypress tree about,
  And, from beneath old wrinkled brows
    Their failing eyes looked out.

  Gray Age and Sickness waiting there
    Through weary night and lingering day —
  Grim as the idols at their side
    And motionless as they.

  Unheeded in the boughs above
    The song of Ceylon's birds was sweet;
  Unseen of them the island flowers
    Bloomed brightly at their feet.

O'er them the tropic night-storm swept,
   The thunder crashed on rock and hill;
The cloud-fire on their eye-balls blazed,
   Yet there they waited still!

What was the world without to them?
   The Moslem's sunset call — the dance
Of Ceylon's maids — the passing gleam
   Of battle-flag and lance?

They waited for that falling leaf,
   Of which the wandering Jogees sing:
Which lends once more to wintry age
   The greenness of its spring.

Oh! — if these poor and blinded ones
   In trustful patience wait to feel
O'er torpid pulse and failing limb
   A youthful freshness steal;

Shall we, who sit beneath that Tree,
   Whose healing leaves of life are shed
In answer to the breath of prayer
   Upon the waiting head:

Not to restore our failing forms,
   And build the spirit's broken shrine,
But, on the fainting SOUL to shed
   A light and life divine:

Shall we grow weary in our watch,
   And murmur at the long delay?
Impatient of our Father's time
   And His appointed way?

Or, shall the stir of outward things
  Allure and claim the Christian's eye,
When on the heathen watcher's ear
  Their powerless murmurs die?

Alas! a deeper test of faith
  Than prison cell or martyr's stake,
The self-abasing watchfulness
  Of silent prayer may make.

We gird us bravely to rebuke
  Our erring brother in the wrong:
And in the ear of Pride and Power
  Our warning voice is strong.

Easier to smite with Peter's sword,
  Than "watch one hour" in humbling prayer:
Life's "great things," like the Syrian lord
  Our hearts can do and dare.

But oh! we shrink from Jordan's side,
  From waters which alone can save:
And murmur for Abana's banks
  And Pharpar's brighter wave.

Oh, Thou, who in the garden's shade
  Didst wake Thy weary ones again,
Who slumbered at that fearful hour
  Forgetful of Thy pain;

Bend o'er us now, as over them,
  And set our sleep-bound spirits free,
Nor leave us slumbering in the watch
  Our souls should keep with Thee!

1841.

A DREAM OF SUMMER.

BLAND as the morning breath of June
    The southwest breezes play;
And, through its haze, the winter noon
    Seems warm as summer's day.
The snow-plumed Angel of the North
    Has dropped his icy spear;
Again the mossy earth looks forth,
    Again the streams gush clear.

The fox his hillside cell forsakes,
    The muskrat leaves his nook,
The bluebird in the meadow brakes
    Is singing with the brook.
"Bear up, oh mother Nature!" cry
    Bird, breeze, and streamlet free;
"Our winter voices prophesy
    Of summer days to thee!"

So, in those winters of the soul,
    By bitter blasts and drear
O'erswept from Memory's frozen pole,
    Will sunny days appear.
Reviving Hope and Faith, they show
    The soul its living powers,
And how beneath the winter's snow
    Lie germs of summer flowers!

The Night is mother of the Day,
    The Winter of the Spring,
And ever upon old Decay
    The greenest mosses cling.
Behind the cloud the starlight lurks,
    Through showers the sunbeams fall;
For God, who loveth all His works,
    Has left His Hope with all!

4th 1st month, 1847.

———◆◆———

TO ——,

WITH A COPY OF WOOLMAN'S JOURNAL.[1]

MAIDEN! with the fair brown tresses
    'Shading o'er thy dreamy eye,
Floating on thy thoughtful forehead
    Cloud wreaths of its sky.

Youthful years and maiden beauty,
    Joy with them should still abide —
Instinct take the place of Duty —
    Love, not Reason, guide.

Ever in the New rejoicing,
    Kindly beckoning back the Old,
Turning, with a power like Midas,
    All things into gold.

[2] "Get the writings of John Woolman by heart."—*Essays of Elia.*

And the passing shades of sadness
    Wearing even a welcome guise,
As when some bright lake lies open
    To the sunny skies;

Every wing of bird above it,
    Every light cloud floating on,
Glitters like that flashing mirror
    In the self-same sun.

But upon thy youthful forehead
    Something like a shadow lies;
And a serious soul is looking
    From thy earnest eyes.

With an early introversion,
    Through the forms of outward things,
Seeking for the subtle essence,
    And the hidden springs.

Deeper than the gilded surface
    Hath thy wakeful vision seen,
Farther than the narrow present
    Have thy journeyings been.

Thou hast midst Life's empty noises
    Heard the solemn steps of Time,
And the low mysterious voices
    Of another clime.

All the mystery of Being
    Hath upon thy spirit pressed —
Thoughts which, like the Deluge wanderer,
    Find no place of rest:

That which mystic Plato pondered,
    That which Zeno heard with awe,
And the star-rapt Zoroaster
    In his night-watch saw.

From the doubt and darkness springing
    Of the dim, uncertain Past,
Moving to the dark still shadows
    O'er the Future cast,

Early hath Life's mighty question
    Thrilled within thy heart of youth
With a deep and strong beseeching:
    WHAT and WHERE IS TRUTH?

Hollow creed and ceremonial,
    Whence the ancient life hath fled,
Idle faith unknown to action,
    Dull and cold and dead.

Oracles, whose wire-worked meanings
    Only wake a quiet scorn, —
Not from these thy seeking spirit
    Hath its answer drawn.

But, like some tired child at even,
    On thy mother Nature's breast,
Thou, methinks, art vainly seeking
    Truth, and peace, and rest.

O'er that mother's rugged features
    Thou art throwing Fancy's veil,
Light and soft as woven moonbeams,
    Beautiful and frail!

O'er the rough chart of Existence,
  Rocks of sin and wastes of woe,
Soft airs breathe, and green leaves tremble,
  And cool fountains flow.

And to thee an answer cometh
  From the earth and from the sky,
And to thee the hills and waters
  And the stars reply.

But a soul-sufficing answer
  Hath no outward origin;
More than Nature's many voices
  May be heard within.

Even as the great Augustine
  Questioned earth and sea and sky,[1]
And the dusty tomes of learning
  And old poesy.

But his earnest spirit needed
  More than outward Nature taught —
More than blest the poet's vision
  Or the sage's thought.

Only in the gathered silence
  Of a calm and waiting frame
Light and wisdom as from Heaven
  To the seeker came.

---

[1] August. Sililoq. cap. xxxi., " Interrogavi Terram," etc.

Not to ease and aimless quiet
   Doth that inward answer tend,
But to works of love and duty
   As our being's end, —

Not to idle dreams and trances,
   Length of face, and solemn tone,
But to Faith, in daily striving
   And performance shown.

Earnest toil and strong endeavor
   Of a spirit which within
Wrestles with familiar evil
   And besetting sin;

And without, with tireless vigor,
   Steady heart, and weapon strong,
In the power of truth assailing
   Every form of wrong.

Guided thus, how passing lovely
   Is the track of WOOLMAN'S feet!
And his brief and simple record
   How serenely sweet!

O'er life's humblest duties throwing
   Light the earthling never knew,
Freshening all its dark waste places
   As with Hermon's dew.

All which glows in Pascal's pages —
   All which sainted Guion sought,
Or the blue-eyed German Rahel
   Half-unconscious taught : —

Beauty, such as Goethe pictured,
   Such as Shelley dreamed of, shed
Living warmth and starry brightness
   Round that poor man's head.

Not a vain and cold ideal,
   Not a poet's dream alone,
But a presence warm and real,
   Seen and felt and known.

When the red right hand of slaughter
   Moulders with the steel it swung,
When the name of seer and poet
   Dies on Memory's tongue,

All bright thoughts and pure shall gather
   Round that meek and suffering one —
Glorious, like the seer-seen angel
   Standing in the sun!

Take the good man's book and ponder
   What its pages say to thee —
Blessed as the hand of healing
   May its lesson be.

If it only serves to strengthen
   Yearnings for a higher good,
For the fount of living waters
   And diviner food;

If the pride of human reason
   Feels its meek and still rebuke,
Quailing like the eye of Peter
   From the Just One's look! —

If with readier ear thou heedest
  What the Inward Teacher saith,
Listening with a willing spirit
  And a child-like faith, —

Thou mayest live to bless the giver,
  Who himself but frail and weak,
Would at least the highest welfare
  Of another seek;

And his gift, though poor and lowly
  It may seem to other eyes,
Yet may prove an angel holy
  In a pilgrim's guise.

1840.

LEGGETT'S MONUMENT.

"Ye build the tombs of the prophets."— HOLY WRIT.

YES— pile the marble o'er him!   It is well
  That ye who mocked him in his long stern strife,
  And planted in the pathway of his life
The ploughshares of your hatred hot from hell,
  Who clamored down the bold reformer when
  He pleaded for his captive fellow-men,
Who spurned him in the market-place, and sought
  Within thy walls, St. Tammany, to bind
In party chains the free and honest thought,
  The angel utterance of an upright mind, —
Well is it now that o'er his grave ye raise
The stony tribute of your tardy praise,
For not alone that pile shall tell to Fame
Of the brave heart beneath, but of the builders' shame!

1841.

THE ANGELS OF BUENA VISTA.

[A LETTER-WRITER from Mexico states that, at the terrible
fight of Buena Vista, MEXICAN women were seen hovering
near the field of death, for the purpose of giving aid and
succor to the wounded. One poor woman was found surrounded by the maimed and suffering of both armies, minister-
ing to the wants of AMERICANS as well as MEXICANS, with
impartial tenderness.]

SPEAK and tell us, our Ximena, looking northward
        far away,
O'er the camp of the invaders, o'er the Mexican
        array,
Who is losing? who is winning? are they far or
        come they near?
Look abroad, and tell us, sister, whither rolls the
        storm we hear.

"Down the hills of Angostura still the storm of
        battle rolls;
Blood is flowing, men are dying; God have mercy
        on their souls!"
Who is losing? who is winning? — "Over hill and
        over plain,
I see but smoke of cannon clouding through the
        mountain rain."

Holy Mother! keep our brothers! Look, Ximena,
        look once more:
"Still I see the fearful whirlwind rolling darkly as
        before,

Bearing on, in strange confusion, friend and foeman,
   foot and horse,
Like some wild and troubled torrent sweeping down
   its mountain course."

Look forth once more, Ximena! "Ah! the smoke
   has rolled away;
And I see the Northern rifles gleaming down the
   ranks of gray.
Hark! that sudden blast of bugles! there the troop
   of Minon wheels;
There the Northern horses thunder, with the cannon
   at their heels.

"Jesu, pity! how it thickens! now retreat and now
   advance!
Right against the blazing cannon shivers Puebla's
   charging lance!
Down they go, the brave young riders; horse and
   foot together fall;
Like a ploughshare in the fallow, through them
   plough the Northern ball."

Nearer came the storm and nearer, rolling fast and
   frightful on:
Speak, Ximena, speak and tell us, who has lost, and
   who has won?
"Alas! alas! I know not; friend and foe together
   fall,
O'er the dying rush the living: pray, my sisters, for
   them all!"

"Lo! the wind the smoke is lifting: Blessed Mother,
    save my brain!
I can see the wounded crawling slowly out from
    heaps of slain.
Now they stagger, blind and bleeding; now they
    fall, and strive to rise;
Hasten, sisters, haste and save them, lest they die
    before our eyes!"

"Oh my heart's love! oh my dear one! lay thy poor
    head on my knee;
Dost thou know the lips that kiss thee? Canst thou
    hear me? canst thou see?
Oh, my husband, brave and gentle! oh, my Bernal,
    look once more
On the blessed cross before thee! mercy! mercy! all
    is o'er!"

Dry thy tears, my poor Ximena; lay thy dear one
    down to rest;
Let his hands be meekly folded, lay the cross upon
    his breast;
Let his dirge be sung hereafter, and his funeral
    masses said;
To-day, thou poor bereaved one, the living ask thy
    aid.

Close beside her, faintly moaning, fair and young, a
    soldier lay,
Torn with shot and pierced with lances, bleeding
    slow his life away;

But, as tenderly before him, the lorn Ximena
    knelt,
She saw the Northern eagle shining on his pistol
    belt.

With a stifled cry of horror straight she turned away
    her head;
With a sad and bitter feeling looked she back upon
    her dead;
But she heard the youth's low moaning, and his
    struggling breath of pain,
And she raised the cooling water to his parching lips
    again.

Whispered low the dying soldier, pressed her hand
    and faintly smiled:
Was that pitying face his mother's? did she watch
    beside her child?
All his stranger words with meaning her woman's
    heart supplied;
With her kiss upon his forehead, " Mother!" mur-
    mured he, and died!

" A bitter curse upon them, poor boy, who led thee
    forth,
From some gentle, sad-eyed mother, weeping, lonely,
    in the North!"
Spake the mournful Mexic woman, as she laid him
    with her dead,
And turned to soothe the living, and bind the wounds
    which bled.

Look forth once more, Ximena! "Like a cloud
    before the wind
Rolls the battle down the mountains, leaving blood
    and death behind;
Ah! they plead in vain for mercy; in the dust the
    wounded strive;
Hide your faces, holy angels! oh, thou Christ of
    God, forgive!"

Sink, oh Night, among thy Mountains! let the cool,
    gray shadows fall;
Dying brothers, fighting demons, drop thy curtain
    over all!
Through the thickening winter twilight, wide apart
    the battle rolled,
In its sheath the sabre rested, and the cannon's lips
    grew cold.

But the noble Mexic women still their holy task pursued,
Through that long, dark night of sorrow, worn and
    faint and lacking food;
Over weak and suffering brothers, with a tender care
    they hung,
And the dying foeman blessed them in a strange
    and Northern tongue.

Not wholly lost, oh Father! is this evil world of ours;
Upward, through its blood and ashes, spring afresh
    the Eden flowers;
From its smoking hell of battle, Love and Pity
    send their prayer,
And still thy white-winged angels hover dimly in our
    air!

1847.

FORGIVENESS.

My heart was heavy, for its trust had been
   Abused, its kindness answered with foul wrong;
So, turning gloomily from my fellow-men,
   One summer Sabbath day I strolled among
The green mounds of the village burial place :
   Where, pondering how all human love and hate
   Find one sad level — and how, soon or late,
Wronged and wrong-doer, each with meekened face,
   And cold hands folded over a still heart,
Pass the green threshold of our common grave,
   Whither all footsteps tend, whence none depart,
Awed for myself, and pitying my race,
Our common sorrow, like a mighty wave,
Swept all my pride away, and trembling I forgave!

1846.

BARCLAY OF URY.

[Among the earliest converts to the doctrines of FRIENDS, in Scotland, was BARCLAY, of URY, an old and distinguished soldier, who had fought under GUSTAVUS ADOLPHUS, in Germany. As a Quaker, he became the object of persecution and abuse at the hands of the magistrates and the populace. None bore the indignities of the mob with greater patience and nobleness of soul than this once proud gentleman and soldier. One of his friends, on an occasion of uncommon rudeness, lamented that he should be treated so harshly in his old age, who had been so honored before. "I find more satisfaction," said BARCLAY, "as well as honor, in being thus insulted for my religious principles, than when, a few years ago, it was usual for the magistrates, as I passed the city of Aberdeen, to meet me on the road and conduct me to public entertainment in their hall, and then escort me out again, to gain my favor."]

Up the streets of Aberdeen,
By the kirk and college green,
    Rode the Laird of Ury;
Close behind him, close beside,
Foul of mouth and evil-eyed,
    Pressed the mob in fury.

Flouted him the drunken churl,
Jeered at him the serving girl,
    Prompt to please her master;
And the begging carlin, late
Fed and clothed at Ury's gate,
    Cursed him as he passed her."

Yet, with calm and stately mien,
Up the streets of Aberdeen
    Came he slowly riding;
And, to all he saw and heard
Answering not with bitter word,
    Turning not for chiding.

Came a troop with broadswords swinging,
Bits and bridles sharply ringing,
    Loose and free and froward;
Quoth the foremost, "Ride him down!
Push him! prick him! through the town
    Drive the Quaker coward!"

But from out the thickening crowd
Cried a sudden voice and loud:
 "Barclay! Ho! a Barclay!"
And the old man at his side,
Saw a comrade, battle tried,
 Scarred and sunburned darkly;

Who with ready weapon bare,
Fronting to the troopers there,
 Cried aloud: "God save us!
Call ye coward him who stood
Ankle deep in Lutzen's blood,
 With the brave Gustavus?"

"Nay, I do not need thy sword,
Comrade mine," said Ury's lord;
 "Put it up I pray thee:
Passive to His holy will,
Trust I in my Master still,
 Even though He slay me.

"Pledges of thy love and faith,
Proved on many a field of death,
 Not by me are needed."
Marvelled much that henchman bold,
That his laird, so stout of old,
 Now so meekly pleaded.

"Woe's the day," he sadly said,
With a slowly shaking head,
 And a look of pity;

"Ury's honest lord reviled,
Mock of knave and sport of child,
    In his own good city!

"Speak the word, and, master mine,
As we charged on Tilly's line,
    And his Walloon lancers,
Smiting through their midst we'll teach
Civil look and decent speech
    To these boyish prancers!"

"Marvel not, mine ancient friend,
Like beginning, like the end:"
    Quoth the Laird of Ury,
"Is the sinful servant more
Than his gracious Lord who bore
    Bonds and stripes in Jewry?

"Give me joy that in His name
I can bear, with patient frame,
    All these vain ones offer;
While for them He suffereth long,
Shall I answer wrong with wrong,
    Scoffing with the scoffer?

"Happier I, with loss of all,
Hunted, outlawed, held in thrall,
    With few friends to greet me,
Than when reeve and squire were seen,
Riding out from Aberdeen,
    With bared heads, to meet me.

"When each good wife, o'er and o'er,
Blessed me as I passed her door;
 And the snooded daughter,
Through her casement glancing down,
Smiled on him who bore renown
 From red fields of slaughter.

" Hard to feel the stranger's scoff,
Hard the old friend's falling off,
 Hard to learn forgiving:
But the Lord His own rewards,
And His love with theirs accords,
 Warm and fresh and living.

"Through this dark and stormy night
Faith beholds a feeble light
 Up the blackness streaking;
Knowing God's own time is best,
In a patient hope I rest
 For the full day-breaking!"

So the Laird of Ury said,
Turning slow his horse's head
 Towards the Tolbooth prison,
Where, through iron grates, he heard
Poor disciples of the Word
 Preach of Christ arisen!

Not in vain, Confessor old,
Unto us the tale is told
 Of thy day of trial;

Every age on him, who strays
From its broad and beaten ways,
    Pours its seven-fold vial.

Happy he whose inward ear
Angel comfortings can hear,
    O'er the rabble's laughter;
And, while Hatred's fagots burn,
Glimpses through the smoke discern
    Of the good hereafter.

Knowing this, that never yet
Share of Truth was vainly set
    In the world's wide fallow;
After hands shall sow the seed,
After hands from hill and mead
    Reap the harvests yellow.

Thus, with somewhat of the Seer,
Must the moral pioneer
    From the Future borrow;
Clothe the waste with dreams of grain,
And, on midnight's sky of rain,
    Paint the golden morrow!

1847.

WHAT THE VOICE SAID.

MADDENED by Earth's wrong and evil,
  " Lord!" I cried in sudden ire,
"From thy right hand, clothed with thunder,
  Shake the bolted fire!

"Love is lost, and Faith is dying;
  With the brute the man is sold;
And the dropping blood of labor
  Hardens into gold.

"Here the dying wail of Famine,
  There the battle's groan of pain;
And, in silence, smooth-faced Mammon
  Reaping men like grain.

"'Where is God, that we should fear Him?'
  Thus the earth-born Titans say;
'God! if thou art living, hear us!'
  Thus the weak ones pray.

"Thou, the patient Heaven upbraiding,"
  Spake a solemn Voice within;
"Weary of our Lord's forbearance,
  Art thou free from sin?

"Fearless brow to Him uplifting,
  Canst thou for His thunders call,
Knowing that to guilt's attraction
  Evermore they fall?

"Know'st thou not all germs of evil
  In thy heart await their time?
Not thyself, but God's restraining,
  Stays their growth of crime.

"Could'st thou boast, oh child of weakness!
  O'er the sons of wrong and strife,
Were their strong temptations planted
  In thy path of life?

" Thou hast seen two streamlets gushing
    From one fountain, clear and free,
But by widely varying channels
    Searching for the sea.

" Glideth one through greenest valleys,
    Kissing them with lips still sweet;
One, mad roaring down the mountains,
    Stagnates at their feet.

" Is it choice whereby the Parsee
    Kneels before his mother's fire?
In his black tent did the Tartar
    Choose his wondering sire?

" He alone, whose hand is bounding
    Human power and human will,
Looking through each soul's surrounding,
    Knows its good or ill.

" For thyself, while wrong and sorrow
    Make to thee their strong appeal,
Coward wert thou not to utter
    What the heart must feel.

" Earnest words must needs be spoken
    When the warm heart bleeds or burns
With its scorn of wrong, or pity
    For the wronged, by turns.

" But, by all thy nature's weakness,
    Hidden faults and follies known,
Be thou, in rebuking evil,
    Conscious of thine own.

" Not the less shall stern-eyed Duty
   To thy lips her trumpet set,
But with harsher blasts shall mingle
   Wailings of regret."

Cease not, Voice of holy speaking,
   Teacher sent of God, be near,
Whispering through the day's cool silence,
   Let my spirit hear!

So, when thoughts of evil doers
   Waken scorn or hatred move,
Shall a mournful fellow-feeling
   Temper all with love.

1847.

———◦✦◦———

TO DELAWARE.

Written during the Discussion, in the Legislature of that
State in the Winter of 1846-47, of a Bill for the Abolition of
Slavery.

THRICE welcome to thy sisters of the East,
   To the strong tillers of a rugged home,
With spray-wet locks to Northern winds released,
   And hardy feet o'er-swept by ocean's foam ;
And to the young nymphs of the golden West,
   Whose harvest mantles, fringed with prairie bloom,
Trail in the sunset, — oh, redeemed and blest,
   To the warm welcome of thy sisters come!
Broad Pennsylvania, down her sail-white bay

Shall give thee joy, and Jersey from her plains,
And the great lakes, where echoes free alway
   Moaned never shoreward with the clank of chains,
Shall weave new sun-bows in their tossing spray,
And all their waves keep grateful holiday.
And, smiling on thee through her mountain rains,
   Vermont shall bless thee; and the Granite peaks,
And vast Katahdin o'er his woods, shall wear
Their snow-crowns brighter in the cold keen air;
   And Massachusetts, with her rugged cheeks
O'errun with grateful tears, shall turn to thee,
   When, at thy bidding, the electric wire
   Shall tremble northward with its words of fire:
Glory and praise to God! another State is free!

   1847.

WORSHIP.

["Pure religion and undefiled before God and the Father
is this, To visit the fatherless and widows in their affliction,
and to keep himself unspotted from the world." — *James* i. 27.]

THE Pagan's myths through marble lips are spoken,
   And ghosts of old Beliefs still flit and moan
Round fane and altar overthrown and broken,
   O'er tree-grown barrow and gray ring of stone.

Blind Faith had martyrs in those old high places,
   The Syrian hill grove and the Druid's wood,
With mothers' offering, to the Fiend's embraces,
   Bone of their bone, and blood of their own blood.

Red altars, kindling through that night of error,
  Smoked with warm blood beneath the cruel eye
Of lawless Power and sanguinary Terror,
  Throned on the circle of a pitiless sky;

Beneath whose baleful shadow, overcasting
  All heaven above, and blighting earth below,
The scourge grew red, the lip grew pale with fasting,
  And man's oblation was his fear and woe!

Then through great temples swelled the dismal
      moaning
  Of dirge-like music and sepulchral prayer;
Pale wizard priests, o'er occult symbols droning,
  Swung their white censers in the burdened air:

As if the pomp of rituals, and the savor
  Of gums and spices, could the Unseen One please;
As if His ear could bend, with childish favor,
  To the poor flattery of the organ keys!

Feet red from war fields trod the church aisles holy,
  With trembling reverence; and the oppressor
      there,
Kneeling before his priest, abased and lowly,
  Crushed human hearts beneath his knee of prayer.

Not such the service the benignant Father
  Requireth at His earthly children's hands:
Not the poor offering of vain rites, but rather
  The simple duty man from man demands.

For Earth he asks it: the full joy of Heaven
   Knoweth no change of waning or increase;
The great heart of the Infinite beats even,
   Untroubled flows the river of His peace.

He asks no taper lights, on high surrounding
   The priestly altar and the saintly grave,
No dolorous chant nor organ music sounding,
   Nor incense clouding up the twilight nave.

For he whom Jesus loved hath truly spoken:
   The holier worship which he deigns to bless
Restores the lost, and binds the spirit broken,
   And feeds the widow and the fatherless!

Types of our human weakness and our sorrow!
   Who lives unhaunted by his loved ones dead?
Who, with vain longing, seeketh not to borrow
   From stranger eyes the home lights which have
      fled?

Oh, brother man! fold to thy heart thy brother;
   Where pity dwells, the peace of God is there;
To worship rightly is to love each other,
   Each smile a hymn, each kindly deed a prayer.

Follow with reverent steps the great example
   Of Him whose holy work was "doing good";
So shall the wide earth seem our Father's temple,
   Each loving life a psalm of gratitude.

Then shall all shackles fall; the stormy clangor
  Of wild war music o'er the earth shall cease;
Love shall tread out the baleful fire of anger,
  And in its ashes plant the tree of peace!

   1848.

———◆◆———

THE ALBUM.

THE dark-eyed daughters of the Sun,
  At morn and evening hours,
O'er-hung their graceful shrines alone
  With wreaths of dewy flowers.

Not vainly did those fair ones cull
  Their gifts by stream and wood;
The Good is always beautiful,
  The Beautiful is good!

We live not in their simple day,
  Our Northern blood is cold,
And few the offerings which we lay
  On other shrines than Gold.

With Scripture texts to chill and ban
  The heart's fresh morning hours,
The heavy-footed Puritan
  Goes trampling down the flowers;

Nor thinks of Him who sat of old
  Where Syrian lilies grew,
And from their mingling shade and gold
  A holy lesson drew.

Yet lady, shall this book of thine,
　　Where Love his gifts has brought,
Become to thee a Persian shrine,
　　O'er-hung with flowers of thought.

THE DEMON OF THE STUDY.

THE Brownie sits in the Scotchman's room,
　　And eats his meat and drinks his ale,
And beats the maid with her unused broom,
　　And the lazy lout with his idle flail,
But he sweeps the floor and threshes the corn,
And hies him away ere the break of dawn.

The shade of Denmark fled from the sun,
　　And the Cocklane ghost from the barn-loft cheer,
The Fiend of Faust was a faithful one,
　　Agrippa's demon wrought in fear,
And the devil of Martin Luther sat
By the stout monk's side in social chat.

The Old Man of the Sea, on the neck of him
　　Who seven times crossed the deep,
Twined closely each lean and withered limb,
　　Like the nightmare in one's sleep.
But he drank of the wine, and Sinbad cast
The evil weight from his back at last.

But the demon that cometh day by day
　　To my quiet room and fire-side nook,
Where the casement light falls dim and gray

On faded painting and ancient book,
Is a sorrier one than any whose names
Are chronicled well by good king James.

No bearer of burdens like Caliban,
   No runner of errands like Ariel,
He comes in the shape of a fat old man,
   Without rap of knuckle or pull of bell :
And whence he comes, or whither he goes,
I know as I do of the wind which blows.

A stout old man with a greasy hat
   Slouched heavily down to his dark, red nose,
And two gray eyes enveloped in fat,
   Looking through glasses with iron bows
Read ye, and heed ye, and ye who can,
Guard well your doors from that old man!

He comes with a careless " how d'ye do,"
   And seats himself in my elbow chair ;
And my morning paper and pamphlet new
   Fall forthwith under his special care,
And he wipes his glasses and clears his throat,
And, button by button, unfolds his coat.

And then he reads from paper and book,
   In a low and husky asthmatic tone,
With the stolid sameness of posture and look
   Of one who reads to himself alone ;
And hour after hour on my senses come
That husky wheeze and that dolorous hum.

The price of stocks, the auction sales,
  The poet's song and the lover's glee,
The horrible murders, the seaboard gales,
  The marriage list, and the *jeu d'esprit*,
All reach my ear in the self-same tone, —
I shudder at each, but the fiend reads on!

Oh! sweet as the lapse of water at noon
  O'er the mossy roots of some forest tree,
The sigh of the wind in the woods of June,
  Or sound of flutes o'er a moonlit sea,
Or the low soft music, perchance which seems
To float through the slumbering singer's dreams.

So sweet, so dear is the silvery tone
  Of her in whose features I sometimes look,
As I sit at eve by her side alone,
  And we read by turns from the self-same book —
Some tale perhaps of the olden time,
Some lover's romance or quaint old rhyme.

Then when the story is one of woe, —
  Some prisoner's plaint through his dungeon-bar,
Her blue eye glistens with tears, and low
  Her voice sinks down like a moan afar;
And I seem to hear that prisoner's wail,
And his face looks on me worn and pale.

And when she reads some merrier song,
  Her voice is glad as an April bird's,
And when the tale is of war and wrong,

A trumpet's summons is in her words,
And the rush of the hosts I seem to hear,
And see the tossing of plume and spear! —

Oh, pity me then, when, day by day,
    The stout fiend darkens my parlor door;
And reads me perchance the self-same lay
    Which melted in music the night before,
From lips as the lips of Hylas sweet,
And moved like twin roses which zephyrs meet!

I cross my floor with a nervous tread,
    I whistle and laugh and sing and shout,
I flourish my cane above his head,
    And stir up the fire to roast him out;
I topple the chairs, and drum on the pane,
And press my hands on my ears, in vain!

I've studied Glanville and James the wise,
    And wizard black-letter tomes which treat
Of demons of every name and size,
    Which a Christian man is presumed to meet.
But never a hint and never a line
Can I find of a reading fiend like mine.

I've crossed the Psalter with Brady and Tate,
    And laid the Primer above them all,
I've nailed a horse-shoe over the grate,
    And hung a wig to my parlor wall
Once worn by a learned Judge, they say,
At Salem court in the witchcraft day!

" *Conjuro te, sceleratissime,*
    Abire ad tuum locum! " — still
Like a visible nightmare he sits by me —
    The exorcism has lost its skill ;
And I hear again in my haunted room
The husky wheeze and the dolorous hum !

Ah! — commend me to Mary Magdalen
    With her seven-fold plagues — to the wandering
        Jew,
To the terrors which haunted Orestes when
    The furies his midnight curtains drew,
But charm him off, ye who charm him can,
That reading demon, that fat old man !

    1835.

THE PUMPKIN.

Oh ! greenly and fair in the lands of the sun,
The vines of the gourd and the rich melon run,
And the rock and the tree and the cottage enfold,
With broad leaves all greenness and blossoms all
        gold,
Like that which o'er Nineveh's prophet once grew,
While he waited to know that his warning was true,
And longed for the storm-cloud, and listened in vain
For the rush of the whirlwind and red fire-rain.

On the banks of the Xenil the dark Spanish maiden
Comes up with the fruit of the tangled vine laden ;

And the Creole of Cuba laughs out to behold
Through orange-leaves shining the broad spheres of
      gold ;
Yet with dearer delight from his home in the North,
On the fields of his harvest the Yankee looks forth,
Where crook-necks are coiling and yellow fruit
      shines,
And the sun of September melts down on his vines.

Ah ! — on Thanksgiving Day, from East and from
      West,
From North and from South come the pilgrim and
      guest,
When the gray-haired New Englander sees round
      his board
The old broken links of affection restored,
When the care-wearied man seeks his mother once
      more,
And the worn matron smiles where the girl smiled
      before,
What moistens the lip and what brightens the eye ?
What calls back the past, like the rich Pumpkin pie ?

Oh ! — fruit loved of boyhood ! — the old days re-
      calling,
When wood-grapes were purpling and brown nuts
      were falling !
When wild, ugly faces we carved in its skin,
Glaring out through the dark with a candle within !
When we laughed round the corn-heap, with hearts
      all in tune,
Our chair a broad pumpkin — our lantern the moon,

Telling tales of the fairy who travelled like steam,
In a pumpkin-shell-coach, with two rats for her
    team !

Then thanks for thy present ! — none sweeter or
    better
E'er smoked from an oven or circled a platter !
Fairer hands never wrought at a pastry more fine,
Brighter eyes never watched o'er its baking than
    thine !
And the prayer, which my mouth is too full to ex-
    press,
Swells my heart that thy shadow may never be less ;
That the days of thy lot may be lengthened below,
And the fame of thy worth like a pumpkin-vine
    grow,
And thy life be as sweet, and its last sunset sky
Golden-tinted and fair as thy own Pumpkin Pie !

        1844.

------◆◆◆------

EXTRACT FROM " A NEW ENGLAND
LEGEND."

How has New England's romance fled,
    Even as a vision of the morning !
Its rights foredone — its guardians dead —
Its priestesses, bereft of dread,
    Waking the veriest urchin's scorning ! —
Gone like the Indian wizard's yell
    And fire-dance round the magic rock,

Forgotten like the Druid's spell
    At moonrise by his holy oak !
No more along the shadowy glen,
    Glide the dim ghosts of murdered men ;
No more the unquiet church-yard dead
Glimpse upward from their turfy bed,
    Startling the traveller, late and lone ;
As, on some night of starless weather,
They silently commune together,
    Each sitting on his own head-stone !
The roofless house, decayed, deserted,
Its living tenants all departed,
No longer rings with midnight revel
Of witch, or ghost, or goblin evil ;
No pale, blue flame sends out its flashes
Through creviced roof and shattered sashes ! —
The witch-grass round the hazel spring
May sharply to the night-air sing,
But there no more shall withered hags
Refresh at ease their broom-stick nags,
Or taste those hazel-shadowed waters
As beverage meet for Satan's daughters ;
No more their mimic tones be heard —
The mew of cat — the chirp of bird,
Shrill blending with the hoarser laughter
Of the fell demon following after !

The cautious good-man nails no more
A horse-shoe on his outer door,
Lest some unseemly hag should fit
To his own mouth her bridle-bit —
The good-wife's churn no more refuses

Its wonted culinary uses
Until, with heated needle burned,
The witch has to her place returned !
Our witches are no longer old
And wrinkled beldames, Satan-sold,
But young and gay and laughing creatures,
With the heart's sunshine on their features —
Their sorcery — the light which dances
Where the raised lid unveils its glances ;
Or that low-breathed and gentle tone,
   The music of Love's twilight hours,
Soft, dream-like, as a fairy's moan
   Above her nightly closing flowers,
Sweeter than that which sighed of yore,
Along the charmed Ausonian shore!
Even she, our own weird heroine,
Sole Pythoness of ancient Lynn,
   Sleeps calmly where the living laid her ;
And the wide realm of sorcery,
Left by its latest mistress free,
   Hath found no gray and skilled invader :
So perished Albion's "glammarye,"
   With him in Melrose Abbey sleeping,
His charmed torch beside his knee,
That even the dead himself might see
   The magic scroll within his keeping.
And now our modern Yankee sees
Nor omens, spells, nor mysteries ;
And naught above, below, around,
Of life or death, of sight or sound,
   Whate'er its nature, form, or look,
Excites his terror or surprise —

All seeming to his knowing eyes
Familiar as his "catechise,"
  Or "Webster's Spelling Book."

1833.

HAMPTON BEACH.

THE sunlight glitters keen and bright,
      Where, miles away,
  Lies stretching to my dazzled sight
  A luminous belt, a misty light,
Beyond the dark pine bluffs and wastes of sandy
      gray.

The tremulous shadow of the Sea!
      Against its ground
  Of silvery light, rock, hill, and tree,
  Still as a picture, clear and free,
With varying outline mark the coast for miles
      around.

On — on — we tread with loose-flung rein
      Our seaward way,
  Through dark-green fields and blossoming grain,
  Where the wild brier-rose skirts the lane,
And bends above our heads the flowering locust
      spray.

Ha! like a kind hand on my brow
      Comes this fresh breeze,
  Cooling its dull and feverish glow,
  While through my being seems to flow
The breath of a new life — the healing of the seas!

Now rest we, where this grassy mound
              His feet hath set
In the great waters, which have bound
His granite ankles greenly round
With long and tangled moss, and weeds with cool
              spray wet.

Good-by to Pain and Care!   I take
              Mine ease to-day;
Here where these sunny waters break,
And ripples this keen breeze, I shake
All burdens from the heart, all weary thoughts away.

I draw a freer breath — I seem
              Like all I see —
Waves in the sun — the white-winged gleam
Of sea-birds in the slanting beam —
And far-off sails which flit before the South-wind
              free.

So when Time's veil shall fall asunder,
              The soul may know
No fearful change, nor sudden wonder,
Nor sink the weight of mystery under,
But with the upward rise, and with the vastness
              grow.

And all we shrink from now may seem
              No new revealing;
Familiar as our childhood's stream
Or pleasant memory of a dream,
The loved and cherished Past upon the new life
              stealing.

Serene and mild the untried light
  May have its dawning;
And, as in Summer's northern night
The evening and the dawn unite,
The sunset hues of Time blend with the soul's new
  morning.

I sit alone: in foam and spray
  Wave after wave
Breaks on the rocks which, stern and gray,
Beneath like fallen Titans lay,
Or murmurs hoarse and strong through mossy cleft
  and cave.

What heed I of the dusty land
  And noisy town?
I see the mighty deep expand
From its white line of glimmering sand
To where the blue of heaven on bluer waves shuts
  down!

In listless quietude of mind,
  I yield to all
The change of cloud and wave and wind,
And passive on the flood reclined,
I wander with the waves, and with them rise and
  fall.

But look, thou dreamer! — wave and shore
  In shadow lie;
The night-wind warns me back once more
To where my native hill-tops o'er
Bends like an arch of fire the glowing sunset sky!

So then, beach, bluff, and wave, farewell!
    I bear with me
No token stone nor glittering shell,
But long and oft shall Memory tell
Of this brief thoughtful hour of musing by the Sea

   1843.

LINES,

WRITTEN ON HEARING OF THE DEATH OF SILAS WRIGHT, OF NEW YORK.

As they who, tossing midst the storm at night,
  While turning shoreward, where a beacon shone,
  Meet the walled blackness of the heaven alone,
So, on the turbulent waves of party tossed,
In gloom and tempest, men have seen thy light
  Quenched in the darkness. At thy hour of noon,
While life was pleasant to thy undimmed sight,
And, day by day, within thy spirit grew
A holier hope than young Ambition knew,
As through thy rural quiet, not in vain,
Pierced the sharp thrill of Freedom's cry of pain,
  Man of the millions, thou art lost too soon!
Portents at which the bravest stand aghast —
The birth-throes of a Future, strange and vast,
  Alarm the land; yet thou, so wise and strong,
Suddenly summoned to the burial bed,
  Lapped in its slumbers deep and ever long,
Hear'st not the tumult surging overhead.
Who now shall rally Freedom's scattering host?
Who wear the mantle of the leader lost?

Who stay the march of slavery?   He, whose voice
  Hath called thee from thy task-field, shall not lack
  Yet bolder champions, to beat bravely back
The wrong which, through His poor ones, reaches
      Him :
Yet firmer hands shall Freedom's torch-lights trim,
  And wave them high across the abysmal black,
Till bound, dumb millions there shall see them and
      rejoice.

  10th mo., 1847.

——•◦•——

LINES,

ACCOMPANYING MANUSCRIPTS PRESENTED TO A FRIEND.

'T IS said that in the Holy Land
  The angels of the place have blessed
The pilgrim's bed of desert sand,
  Like Jacob's stone of rest.

That down the hush of Syrian skies
  Some sweet-voiced saint at twilight sings
The song whose holy symphonies
  Are beat by unseen wings ;

Still starting from his sandy bed,
  The way-worn wanderer looks to see
The halo of an angel's head
  Shine through the tamarisk tree.

So through the shadows of my way
  Thy smile hath fallen soft and clear,

So at the weary close of day
　　Hath seemed thy voice of cheer.

That pilgrim pressing to his goal
　　May pause not for the vision's sake,
Yet all fair things within his soul
　　The thought of it shall wake;

The graceful palm tree by the well,
　　Seen on the far horizon's rim;
The dark eyes of the fleet gazelle,
　　Bent timidly on him;

Each pictured saint, whose golden hair
　　Streams sunlike through the convent's gloom;
Pale shrines of martyrs young and fair,
　　And loving Mary's tomb;

And thus each tint or shade which falls
　　From sunset cloud or waving tree,
Along my pilgrim path recalls
　　The pleasant thought of thee.

Of one, in sun and shade the same,
　　In weal and woe my steady friend,
Whatever by that holy name
　　The angels comprehend.

Not blind to faults and follies, thou
　　Hast never failed the good to see,
Nor judged by one unseemly bough
　　The upward-struggling tree.

These light leaves at thy feet I lay —
  Poor common thoughts on common things,
Which time is shaking, day by day,
  Like feathers from his wings —

Chance shootings from a frail life-tree,
  To nurturing care but little known,
Their good was partly learned of thee,
  Their folly is my own.

That tree still clasps the kindly mould,
  Its leaves still drink the twilight dew,
And weaving its pale green with gold,
  Still shines the sunlight through.

There still the morning zephyrs play,
  And there at times the spring bird sings,
And mossy trunk and fading spray
  Are flowered with glossy wings.

Yet, even in genial sun and rain,
  Root, branch, and leaflet fail and fade :
The wanderer on its lonely plain
  Ere long shall miss its shade.

Oh, friend beloved, whose curious skill
  Keeps bright the last year's leaves and flowers,
With warm, glad summer thoughts to fill
  The cold, dark, winter hours!

Pressed on my heart, the leaves I bring
  May well defy the wintry cold,
Until, in Heaven's eternal spring,
  Life's fairer ones unfold.

1847.

THE REWARD.

WHO, looking backward from his manhood's prime,
Sees not the spectre of his misspent time?
        And, through the shade
Of funeral cypress planted thick behind,
Hears no reproachful whisper on the wind
        From his loved dead?

Who bears no trace of passion's evil force?
Who shuns thy sting, oh terrible Remorse? —
        Who does not cast
On the thronged pages of his memory's book,
At times, a sad and half reluctant look,
        Regretful of the Past?

Alas! — the evil which we fain would shun
We do, and leave the wished-for good undone:
        Our strength to-day
Is but to-morrow's weakness, prone to fall;
Poor, blind, unprofitable servants all
        Are we alway.

Yet, who, thus looking backward o'er his years,
Feels not his eyelids wet with grateful tears,
        If he hath been
Permitted, weak and sinful as he was,
To cheer and aid, in some ennobling cause,
        His fellow-men?

If he hath hidden the outcast, or let in
A ray of sunshine to the cell of sin, —
     If he hath lent
Strength to the weak, and, in an hour of need,
Over the suffering, mindless of his creed
       Or home, hath bent,

He has not lived in vain, and while he gives
The praise to Him, in whom he moves and lives,
     With thankful heart;
He gazes backward, and with hope before,
Knowing that from his works he never more
      Can henceforth part.

   1848.

RAPHAEL.[1]

I SHALL not soon forget that sight:
   The glow of Autumn's westering day,
A hazy warmth, a dreamy light,
   On Raphael's picture lay.

It was a simple print I saw,
   The fair face of a musing boy;
Yet while I gazed a sense of awe
   Seemed blending with my joy.

[1] Suggested by a portrait of Raphael, at the age of fifteen, in the possession of Thomas Tracy, of Newburyport.

A simple print : — the graceful flow
　Of boyhood's soft and wavy hair,
And fresh young lip and cheek, and brow
　Unmarked and clear, were there.

Yet through its sweet and calm repose
　I saw the inward spirit shine ;
It was as if before me rose
　The white veil of a shrine.

As if, as Gothland's sage has told,
　The hidden life, the man within,
Dissevered from its frame and mould,
　By mortal eye were seen.

Was it the lifting of that eye,
　The waving of that pictured hand?
Loose as a cloud-wreath on the sky,
　I saw the walls expand.

The narrow room had vanished, — space
　Broad, luminous, remained alone,
Through which all hues and shapes of grace
　And beauty looked or shone.

Around the mighty master came
　The marvels which his pencil wrought,
Those miracles of power whose fame
　Is wide as human thought.

There drooped thy more than mortal face,
  Oh Mother, beautiful and mild!
Enfolding in one dear embrace
  Thy Saviour and Thy Child!

The rapt brow of the Desert John;
  The awful glory of that day,
When all the Father's brightness shone
  Through manhood's veil of clay.

And, midst gray prophet forms, and wild
  Dark visions of the days of old,
How sweetly woman's beauty smiled
  Through locks of brown and gold!

There Fornarina's fair young face
  Once more upon her lover shone,
Whose model of an angel's grace
  He borrowed from her own.

Slow passed that vision from my view,
  But not the lesson which it taught;
The soft, calm shadows which it threw
  Still rested on my thought:

The truth, that painter, bard, and sage,
  Even in Earth's cold and changeful clime,
Plant for their deathless heritage
  The fruits and flowers of time.

We shape ourselves the joy or fear
   Of which the coming life is made,
And fill our Future's atmosphere
   With sunshine or with shade.

The tissue of the Life to be
   We weave with colors all our own,
And in the field of Destiny
   We reap as we have sown.

Still shall the soul around it call
   The shadows which it gathered here,
And painted on the eternal wall
   The Past shall reappear.

Think ye the notes of holy song
   On Milton's tuneful ear have died?
Think ye that Raphael's angel throng
   Has vanished from his side?

Oh no! — We live our life again:
   Or warmly touched or coldly dim
The pictures of the Past remain, —
   Man's works shall follow him!

1842.

THE KNIGHT OF ST. JOHN.

Ere down yon blue Carpathian hills
    The sun shall sink again!
Farewell to life and all its ills,
    Farewell to cell and chain.

These prison shades are dark and cold, —
    But, darker far than they,
The shadow of a sorrow old
    Is on my heart alway.

For since the day when Warkworth wood
    Closed o'er my steed and I,
An alien from my name and blood,
    A weed cast out to die, —

When, looking back in sunset light,
    I saw her turret gleam,
And from its casement, far and white,
    Her sign of farewell stream,

Like one who from some desert shore
    Doth home's green isles descry,
And, vainly longing, gazes o'er
    The waste of wave and sky;

So from the desert of my fate
    I gaze across the past;
Forever on life's dial-plate
    The shade is backward cast!

I've wandered wide from shore to shore,
   I've knelt at many a shrine;
And bowed me to the rocky floor
   Where Bethlehem's tapers shine;

And by the Holy Sepulchre
   I've pledged my knightly sword
To Christ, his blessed Church, and her,
   The Mother of our Lord.

Oh, vain the vow, and vain the strife!
   How vain do all things seem!
My soul is in the past, and life
   To-day is but a dream!

In vain the penance strange and long,
   And hard for flesh to bear;
The prayer, the fasting, and the thong,
   And sackcloth shirt of hair.

The eyes of memory will not sleep, —
   Its ears are open still;
And vigils with the past they keep
   Against my feeble will.

And still the loves and joys of old
   Do evermore uprise;
I see the flow of locks of gold,
   The shine of loving eyes!

Ah me! upon another's breast
  Those golden locks recline;
I see upon another rest
  The glance that once was mine!

"O faithless Priest! — O perjured knight!"
  I hear the Master cry;
"Shut out the vision from thy sight,
  Let Earth and Nature die!

"The Church of God is now thy spouse,
  And thou the bridegroom art;
Then let the burden of thy vows
  Crush down thy human heart!"

In vain! This heart its grief must know,
  Till life itself hath ceased,
And falls beneath the self-same blow,
  The lover and the priest!

O pitying Mother! souls of light,
  And saints, and martyrs old!
Pray for a weak and sinful knight,
  A suffering man uphold.

Then let the Paynim work his will,
  And death unbind my chain,
Ere down yon blue Carpathian hill
  The sun shall fall again.

1843.

AUTUMN THOUGHTS.

FROM " MARGARET SMITH'S JOURNAL."

GONE hath the Spring, with all its flowers,
 And gone the Summer's pomp and show,
And Autumn, in his leafless bowers,
 Is waiting for the Winter's snow.

I said to Earth, so cold and gray,
 "An emblem of myself thou art : "
" Not so," the Earth did seem to say,
 " For Spring shall warm my frozen heart."

" I soothe my wintry sleep with dreams
 Of warmer sun and softer rain,
And wait to hear the sound of streams
 And songs of merry birds again.

" But thou, from whom the Spring hath gone,
 For whom the flowers no longer blow,
Who standest blighted and forlorn,
 Like Autumn waiting for the snow :

" No hope is thine of sunnier hours,
 Thy Winter shall no more depart ;
No Spring revive thy wasted flowers,
 Nor Summer warm thy frozen heart."

1849.

SONGS OF LABOR.

———◦◦◦———

DEDICATION.

I WOULD the gift I offer here
   Might graces from thy favor take,
And, seen through Friendship's atmosphere,
On softened lines and coloring, wear
The unaccustomed light of beauty, for thy sake.

Few leaves of Fancy's spring remain :
   But what I have I give to thee, —
The o'er-sunned bloom of summer's plain,
And paler flowers, the latter rain
Calls from the westering slope of life's autumnal lea.

Above the fallen groves of green,
   Where youth's enchanted forest stood,
The dry and wasting roots between,
A sober after-growth is seen,
As springs the pine where falls the gay-leafed maple
     wood !

Yet birds will sing, and breezes play
   Their leaf-harps in the sombre tree;
And through the bleak and wintry day
It keeps its steady green alway, —
So even my after-thoughts may have a charm for
    thee.

Art's perfect forms no moral need,
   And beauty is its own excuse; [1]
But for the dull and flowerless weed
Some healing virtue still must plead,
And the rough ore must find its honors in its use.

So haply these, my simple lays
   Of homely toil, may serve to show
The orchard bloom and tasselled maize
That skirt and gladden duty's ways,
The unsung beauty hid life's common things below!

Haply from them the toiler, bent
   Above his forge or plough, may gain
A manlier spirit of content,
And feel that life is wisest spent
Where the strong working hand makes strong the
    working brain.

---

[1] For the idea of this line, I am indebted to Emerson, in
his inimitable sonnet to the Rhodora: —

    " If eyes were made for seeing,
    Then beauty is its own excuse for being."

The doom which to the guilty pair
   Without the walls of Eden came,
Transforming sinless ease to care
And rugged toil, no more shall bear
The burden of old crime, or mark of primal shame.

A blessing now — a curse no more;
   Since He, whose name we breathe with awe,
The coarse mechanic vesture wore, —
A poor man toiling with the poor,
ın labor, as in prayer, fulfilling the same law.

  1850.

THE SHIP-BUILDERS.

THE sky is ruddy in the East,
   The earth is gray below,
And, spectral in the river-mist,
   The ship's white timbers show.
Then let the sounds of measured stroke
   And grating saw begin;
The broad-axe to the gnarléd oak,
   The mallet to the pin!

Hark! — roars the bellows, blast on blast,
   The sooty smithy jars,
And fire-sparks, rising far and fast,
   Are fading with the stars.
All day for us the smith shall stand
   Beside that flashing forge;
All day for us his heavy hand
   The groaning anvil scourge.

From far-off hills, the panting team
   For us is toiling near;
For us the raftsmen down the stream
   Their island barges steer.
Rings out for us the axe-man's stroke
   In forests old and still, —
For us the century-circled oak
   Falls crashing down his hill.

Up — up! — in nobler toil than ours
   No craftsmen bear a part:
We make of Nature's giant powers
   The slaves of human Art.
Lay rib to rib and beam to beam,
   And drive the treenails free;
Nor faithless joint nor yawning seam
   Shall tempt the searching sea!

Where'er the keel of our good ship
   The sea's rough field shall plough —
Where'er her tossing spars shall drip
   With salt-spray caught below —
That ship must heed her master's beck,
   Her helm obey his hand,
And seamen tread her reeling deck
   As if they trod the land.

Her oaken ribs the vulture-beak
   Of Northern ice may peel;
The sunken rock and coral peak
   May grate along her keel;

And know we well the painted shell
  We give to wind and wave,
Must float, the sailor's citadel,
  Or sink, the sailor's grave!

Ho! — strike away the bars and blocks,
  And set the good ship free!
Why lingers on these dusty rocks
  The young bride of the sea?
Look! how she moves adown the grooves,
  In graceful beauty now!
How lowly on the breast she loves
  Sinks down her virgin prow!

God bless her! wheresoe'er the breeze
  Her snowy wing shall fan,
Aside the frozen Hebrides,
  Or sultry Hindostan!
Where'er, in mart or on the main,
  With peaceful flag unfurled,
She helps to wind the silken chain
  Of commerce round the world!

Speed on the ship! — But let her bear
  No merchandise of sin,
No groaning cargo of despair
  Her roomy hold within.
No Lethean drug for Eastern lands,
  Nor poison-draught for ours;
But honest fruits of toiling hands
  And Nature's sun and showers.

Be hers the Prairie's golden grain,
  The Desert's golden sand,
The clustered fruits of sunny Spain,
  The spice of Morning land!
Her pathway on the open main
  May blessings follow free,
And glad hearts welcome back again
  Her white sails from the sea!

1846.

THE SHOEMAKERS.

Ho! workers of the old time styled
  The Gentle Craft of Leather!
Young brothers of the ancient guild,
  Stand forth once more together!
Call out again your long array,
  In the olden merry manner!
Once more, on gay St. Crispin's day,
  Fling out your blazoned banner!

Rap, rap! upon the well-worn stone
  How falls the polished hammer!
Rap, rap! the measured sound has grown
  A quick and merry clamor.
Now shape the sole! now deftly curl
  The glossy vamp around it,
And bless the while the bright-eyed girl
  Whose gentle fingers bound it!

For you, along the Spanish main
    A hundred keels are ploughing;
For you, the Indian on the plain
    His lasso-coil is throwing;
For you, deep glens with hemlock dark
    The woodman's fire is lighting;
For you, upon the oak's gray bark
    The woodman's axe is smiting.

For you, from Carolina's pine
    The rosin-gum is stealing;
For you, the dark-eyed Florentine
    Her silken skein is reeling;
For you, the dizzy goat-herd roams
    His rugged Alpine ledges;
For you, round all her shepherd homes,
    Bloom England's thorny hedges.

The foremost still, by day or night,
    On moated mound or heather,
Where'er the need of trampled right
    Brought toiling men together;
Where the free burghers from the wall
    Defied the mail-clad master,
Than yours, at Freedom's trumpet-call,
    No craftsmen rallied faster.

Let foplings sneer, let fools deride —
    Ye heed no idle scorner;
Free hands and hearts are still your pride,
    And duty done, your honor.

Ye dare to trust, for honest fame,
　The jury Time empanels,
And leave to truth each noble name
　Which glorifies your annals.

Thy songs, Hans Sachs, are living yet,
　In strong and hearty German;
And Bloomfield's lay, and Gifford's wit,
　And patriot fame of Sherman;
Still from his book, a mystic seer,
　The soul of Behmen teaches,
And England's priestcraft shakes to hear
　Of Fox's leathern breeches.

The foot is yours; where'er it falls,
　It treads your well-wrought leather,
On earthern floor, in marble halls,
　On carpet, or on heather.
Still there the sweetest charm is found
　Of matron grace or vestal's,
As Hebe's foot bore nectar round
　Among the old celestials!

Rap! rap! — your stout and bluff brogan,
　With footsteps slow and weary,
May wander where the sky's blue span
　Shuts down upon the prairie.
On Beauty's foot, your slippers glance,
　By Saratoga's fountains,
Or twinkle down the summer dance
　Beneath the Crystal Mountains!

The red brick to the mason's hand,
  The brown earth to the tiller's,
The shoe in yours shall wealth command,
  Like fairy Cinderella's!
As they who shunned the household maid
  Beheld the crown upon her,
So all shall see your toil repaid
  With hearth and home and honor.

Then let the toast be freely quaffed,
  In water cool and brimming —
"All honor to the good old Craft,
  Its merry men and women!"
Call out again your long array,
  In the old time's pleasant manner;
Once more, on gay St. Crispin's day,
  Fling out his blazoned banner!

1846.

THE DROVERS.

THROUGH heat and cold, and shower and sun
  Still onward cheerly driving!
There's life alone in duty done,
  And rest alone in striving.
But see! the day is closing cool,
  The woods are dim before us;
The white fog of the way-side pool
  Is creeping slowly o'er us.

The night is falling, comrades mine,
　　Our foot-sore beasts are weary,
And through yon elms the tavern sign
　　Looks out upon us cheery.
The landlord beckons from his door,
　　His beechen fire is glowing;
These ample barns, with feed in store,
　　Are filled to overflowing.

From many a valley frowned across
　　By brows of rugged mountains;
From hill-sides where, through spongy moss,
　　Gush out the river fountains;
From quiet farm-fields, green and low,
　　And bright with blooming clover;
From vales of corn the wandering crow
　　No richer hovers over;

Day after day our way has been,
　　O'er many a hill and hollow;
By lake and stream, by wood and glen,
　　Our stately drove we follow.
Through dust-clouds rising thick and dun,
　　As smoke of battle o'er us,
Their white horns glisten in the sun,
　　Like plumes and crests before us.

We see them slowly climb the hill,
　　As slow behind it sinking;
Or, thronging close, from road-side rill.
　　Or sunny lakelet, drinking.

Now crowding in the narrow road,
　　In thick and struggling masses,
They glare upon the teamster's load,
　　Or rattling coach that passes.

Anon, with toss of horn and tail,
　　And paw of hoof, and bellow,
They leap some farmer's broken pale,
　　O'er meadow-close or fallow.
Forth comes the startled good-man; forth
　　Wife, children, house-dog, sally,
Till once more on their dusty path
　　The baffled truants rally.

We drive no starvelings, scraggy grown,
　　Loose-legged, and ribbed and bony,
Like those who grind their noses down
　　On pastures bare and stony —
Lank oxen, rough as Indian dogs,
　　And cows too lean for shadows,
Disputing feebly with the frogs
　　The crop of saw-grass meadows!

In our good drove, so sleek and fair,
　　No bones of leanness rattle;
No tottering hide-bound ghosts are there,
　　Or Pharaoh's evil cattle.
Each stately beeve bespeaks the hand
　　That fed him unrepining;
The fatness of a goodly land
　　In each dun hide is shining.

We've sought them where, in warmest nooks,
  The freshest feed is growing,
By sweetest springs and clearest brooks
  Through honeysuckle flowing;
Wherever hill-sides, sloping south,
  Are bright with early grasses,
Or, tracking green the lowland's drouth,
  The mountain streamlet passes.

But now the day is closing cool,
  The woods are dim before us,
The white fog of the way-side pool
  Is creeping slowly o'er us.
The cricket to the frog's bassoon
  His shrillest time is keeping;
The sickle of yon setting moon
  The meadow-mist is reaping.

The night is falling, comrades mine,
  Our foot-sore beasts are weary,
And through yon elms the tavern sign
  Looks out upon us cheery.
To-morrow, eastward with our charge
  We'll go to meet the dawning,
Ere yet the pines of Kéarsarge
  Have seen the sun of morning.

When snow-flakes o'er the frozen earth,
  Instead of birds, are flitting;
When children throng the glowing hearth,
  And quiet wives are knitting;

While in the fire-light strong and clear
    Young eyes of pleasure glisten,
To tales of all we see and hear
    The ears of home shall listen.

By many a Northern lake and hill,
    From many a mountain pasture,
Shall Fancy play the Drover still,
    And speed the long night faster.
Then let us on, through shower and sun,
    And heat and cold, be driving;
There's life alone in duty done,
    And rest alone in striving.

1847.

THE FISHERMEN.

HURRAH! the seaward breezes
    Sweep down the bay amain;
Heave up, my lads, the anchor!
    Run up the sail again!
Leave to the lubber landsmen
    The rail-car and the steed;
The stars of heaven shall guide us,
    The breath of heaven shall speed.

From the hill-top looks the steeple,
    And the light-house from the sand;
And the scattered pines are waving
    Their farewell from the land.

One glance, my lads, behind us,
　　For the homes we leave one sigh,
Ere we take the change and chances
　　Of the ocean and the sky.

Now brothers, for the icebergs
　　Of frozen Labrador,
Floating spectral in the moonshine,
　　Along the low, black shore!
Where like snow the gannet's feathers
　　Of Brador's rocks are shed,
And the noisy murr are flying,
　　Like black scuds, overhead;

Where in mist the rock is hiding,
　　And the sharp reef lurks below,
And the white squall smites in summer,
　　And the autumn tempests blow;
Where, through gray and rolling vapor,
　　From evening unto morn,
A thousand boats are hailing,
　　Horn answering unto horn.

Hurrah! for the Red Island,
　　With the white cross on its crown!
Hurrah! for Meccatina,
　　And its mountains bare and brown!
Where the Caribou's tall antlers
　　O'er the dwarf-wood freely toss,
And the footstep of the Mickmack
　　Has no sound upon the moss.

There we'll drop our lines, and gather
   Old Ocean's treasures in,
Where'er the mottled mackerel
   Turns up a steel-dark fin.
The sea's our field of harvest,
   Its scaly tribes our grain;
We'll reap the teeming waters
   As at home they reap the plain!

Our wet hands spread the carpet,
   And light the hearth of home;
From our fish, as in the old time,
   The silver coin shall come.
As the demon fled the chamber
   Where the fish of Tobit lay,
So ours from all our dwellings
   Shall frighten Want away.

Though the mist upon our jackets
   In the bitter air congeals,
And our lines wind stiff and slowly
   From off the frozen reels;
Though the fog be dark around us,
   And the storm blow high and loud,
We will whistle down the wild wind,
   And laugh beneath the cloud!

In the darkness as in daylight,
   On the water as on land,
God's eye is looking on us,
   And beneath us is his hand!

Death will find us soon or later,
 On the deck or in the cot;
And we cannot meet him better
 Than in working out our lot.

Hurrah! — hurrah! — the west wind
 Comes freshening down the bay,
The rising sails are filling —
 Give way, my lads, give way!
Leave the coward landsman clinging
 To the dull earth, like a weed —
The stars of heaven shall guide us,
 The breath of heaven shall speed!

1845.

THE HUSKERS.

It was late in mild October, and the long autumnal
 rain
Had left the summer harvest-fields all green with
 grass again;
The first sharp frosts had fallen, leaving all the
 woodlands gay
With the hues of summer's rainbow, or the meadow-
 flowers of May.

Through a thin, dry mist, that morning, the sun
 rose broad and red,
At first a rayless disc of fire, he brightened as he
 sped;

Yet, even his noontide glory fell chastened and
  subdued,
On the corn-fields and the orchards, and softly pictured wood.

And all that quiet afternoon, slow sloping to the
  night,
He wove with golden shuttle the haze with yellow
  light ;
Slanting through the painted beeches, he glorified
  the hill ;
And, beneath it, pond and meadow lay brighter,
  greener still.

And shouting boys in woodland haunts caught
  glimpses of that sky,
Flecked by the many-tinted leaves, and laughed,
  they knew not why ;
And school-girls, gay with aster-flowers, beside the
  meadow brooks,
Mingled the glow of autumn with the sunshine of
  sweet looks.

From spire and barn, looked westerly the patient
  weather-cocks ;
But even the birches on the hill stood motionless as
  rocks.
No sound was in the woodlands, save the squirrel's
  dropping shell,
And the yellow leaves among the boughs, low
  rustling as they fell.

The summer grains were harvested; the stubble-
 fields lay dry,
Where June winds rolled, in light and shade, the
 pale-green waves of rye ;
But still, on gentle hill-slopes, in valleys fringed
 with wood,
Ungathered, bleaching in the sun, the heavy corn
 crop stood.

Bent low, by autumn's wind and rain, through
 husks that, dry and sere,
Unfolded from their ripened charge, shone out the
 yellow ear ;
Beneath, the turnip lay concealed, in many a verdant
 fold,
And glistened in the slanting light the pumpkin's
 sphere of gold.

There wrought the busy harvesters; and many a
 creaking wain
Bore slowly to the long barn-floor its load of husk
 and grain ;
Till broad and red, as when he rose, the sun sank
 down, at last,
And like a merry guest's farewell, the day in brightness passed.

And lo! as through the western pines, on meadow,
 stream and pond,
Flamed the red radiance of a sky, set all afire
 beyond,

Slowly o'er the Eastern sea-bluffs a milder glory
    shone,
And the sunset and the moonrise were mingled into
    one!

As thus into the quiet night the twilight lapsed
    away,
And deeper in the brightening moon the tranquil
    shadows lay;
From many a brown old farm-house, and hamlet
    without name,
Their milking and their home-tasks done, the merry
    huskers came.

Swung o'er the heaped-up-harvest, from pitchforks
    in the mow,
Shone dimly down the lanterns on the pleasant
    scene below;
The growing pile of husks behind, the golden ears
    before,
And laughing eyes and busy hands and brown
    cheeks glimmering o'er.

Half hidden in a quiet nook, serene of look and
    heart,
Talking their old times over, the old men sat
    apart;
While, up and down the unhusked pile, or nestling
    in its shade,
At hide-and-seek, with laugh and shout, the happy
    children played.

Urged by the good host's daughter, a maiden young
    and fair,
Lifting to light her sweet blue eyes and pride of soft
    brown hair,
The master of the village school, sleek of hair and
    smooth of tongue,
To the quaint tune of some old psalm, a husking-
    ballad sung.

    1847.

THE CORN SONG.

HEAP high the farmer's wintry hoard!
    Heap high the golden corn!
No richer gift has Autumn poured
    From out her lavish horn!

Let other lands, exulting, glean
    The apple from the pine,
The orange from its glossy green,
    The cluster from the vine;

We better love the hardy gift
    Our rugged vales bestow,
To cheer us when the storm shall drift
    Our harvest fields with snow.

Through vales of grass and meads of flowers,
    Our ploughs their furrows made,
While on the hills the sun and showers
    Of changeful April played.

We dropped the seed o'er hill and plain,
   Beneath the sun of May,
And frightened from our sprouting grain
   The robber crows away.

All through the long, bright days of June,
   Its leaves grew green and fair,
And waved in hot midsummer's noon
   Its soft and yellow hair.

And now, with Autumn's moonlit eves,
   Its harvest time has come,
We pluck away the frosted leaves,
   And bear the treasure home.

There, richer than the fabled gift
   Apollo showered of old,
Fair hands the broken grain shall sift,
   And knead its meal of gold.

Let vapid idlers loll in silk,
   Around their costly board;
Give us the bowl of samp and milk,
   By homespun beauty poured!

Where'er the wide old kitchen hearth
   Sends up its smoky curls,
Who will not thank the kindly earth,
   And bless our farmer girls!

Then shame on all the proud and vain,
    Whose folly laughs to scorn
The blessing of our hardy grain,
    Our wealth of golden corn!

Let earth withhold her goodly root,
    Let mildew blight the rye,
Give to the worm the orchard's fruit,
    The wheat-field to the fly:

But let the good old crop adorn
    The hills our fathers trod;
Still let us, for his golden corn,
    Send up our thanks to God!

1847.

THE LUMBERMEN.

WILDLY round our woodland quarters,
    Sad-voiced Autumn grieves;
Thickly down these swelling waters
    Float his fallen leaves.
Through the tall and naked timber,
    Column-like and old,
Gleam the sunsets of November,
    From their skies of gold.

O'er us, to the southland heading,
    Screams the gray wild-goose;
On the night-frost sounds the treading
    Of the brindled moose.

Noiseless creeping, while we're sleeping,
  Frost his task-work plies ;
Soon, his icy bridges heaping,
  Shall our log-piles rise.

When, with sounds of smothered thunder,
  On some night of rain,
Lake and river break asunder
  Winter's weakened chain,
Down the wild March flood shall bear them
  To the saw-mill's wheel,
Or where Steam, the slave, shall tear them
  With his teeth of steel.

Be it starlight, be it moonlight,
  In these vales below,
When the earliest beams of sunlight
  Streak the mountain's snow,
Crisps the hoar-frost, keen and early,
  To our hurrying feet,
And the forest echoes clearly
  All our blows repeat.

Where the crystal Ambijejis
  Stretches broad and clear,
And Millnoket's pine-black ridges
  Hide the browsing deer :
Where, through lakes and wide morasses,
  Or through rocky walls,
Swift and strong, Penobscot passes
  White with foamy falls ;

Where, through clouds, are glimpses given
    Of Katahdin's sides, —
Rock and forest piled to heaven,
    Torn and ploughed by slides!
Far below, the Indian trapping,
    In the sunshine warm;
Far above, the snow-cloud wrapping
    Half the peak in storm!

Where are mossy carpets better
    Than the Persian weaves,
And than Eastern perfumes sweeter
    Seem the fading leaves;
And a music wild and solemn,
    From the pine-tree's height,
Rolls its vast and sea-like volume
    On the wind of night;

Make we here our camp of winter;
    And, through sleet and snow,
Pitchy knot and beechen splinter
    On our hearth shall glow.
Here, with mirth to lighten duty,
    We shall lack alone
Woman's smile and girlhood's beauty,
    Childhood's lisping tone.

But their hearth is brighter burning
    For our toil to-day;
And the welcome of returning
    Shall our loss repay,

When, like seamen from the waters,
  From the woods we come,
Greeting sisters, wives, and daughters,
  Angels of our home!

Not for us the measured ringing
  From the village spire,
Not for us the Sabbath singing
  Of the sweet-voiced choir:
Ours the old, majestic temple,
  Where God's brightness shines
Down the dome so grand and ample,
  Propped by lofty pines!

Through each branch-enwoven skylight,
  Speaks He in the breeze,
As of old beneath the twilight
  Of lost Eden's trees!
For his ear, the inward feeling
  Needs no outward tongue;
He can see the spirit kneeling
  While the axe is swung.

Heeding truth alone, and turning
  From the false and dim,
Lamp of toil or altar burning
  Are alike to Him.
Strike, then, comrades! — Trade is waiting
  On our rugged toil;
Far ships waiting for the freighting
  Of our woodland spoil!

Ships, whose traffic links these highlands,
　　Bleak and cold, of ours,
With the citron-planted islands
　　Of a clime of flowers;
To our frosts the tribute bringing
　　Of eternal heats;
In our lap of winter flinging
　　Tropic fruits and sweets.

Cheerly, on the axe of labor,
　　Let the sunbeams dance,
Better than the flash of sabre
　　Or the gleam of lance!
Strike!— With every blow is given
　　Freer sun and sky,
And the long-hid earth to heaven
　　Looks, with wondering eye!

Loud behind us grow the murmurs
　　Of the age to come;
Clang of smiths, and tread of farmers,
　　Bearing harvest-home!
Here her virgin lap with treasures
　　Shall the green earth fill;
Waving wheat and golden maize-ears
　　Crown each beechen hill.

Keep who will the city's alleys,
　　Take the smooth-shorn plain, —
Give to us the cedar valleys,
　　Rocks and hills of Maine!

In our North-land, wild and woody,
    Let us still have part;
Rugged nurse and mother sturdy,
    Hold us to thy heart!

O! our free hearts beat the warmer
    For thy breath of snow;
And our tread is all the firmer
    For thy rocks below.
Freedom, hand in hand with labor,
    Walketh strong and brave;
On the forehead of his neighbor
    No man writeth Slave!

Lo, the day breaks! old Katahdin's
    Pine-trees show its fires,
While from these dim forest gardens
    Rise their blackened spires.
Up, my comrades! up and doing!
    Manhood's rugged play
Still renewing, bravely hewing
    Through the world our way!

1845.